INDIANA
AND THE
GREAT FLOOD
OF 1913

NANCY M. GERMANO

THE
History
PRESS

Published by The History Press
Charleston, SC
www.historypress.com

Back cover: A postcard showing people in upstairs windows of flooded buildings and a boat on Walnut Street in Lawrenceburg, circa 1913. *Collection of Jenny Awad, Dearborn County State Historian.*

First published 2021

ISBN 9781540246790

Library of Congress Control Number: 2020951677

CONTENTS

INTRODUCTION

In March 1913, severe weather moved across the Midwest in the United States, making national headlines. Indiana residents had experienced many floods, but the Great Flood of 1913 set new records for water levels, lives lost and damage caused. According to a U.S. Congressional report, the flood stood out from its predecessors because of the exceptional magnitude and intensity of its storms and because the greatest damage it caused occurred along tributaries, which had not been the case in the past. The U.S. Weather Bureau reported a rain total in Indianapolis in excess of six inches during the period beginning March 23 and March 27, 1913. While six inches of rain over a five-day period is not an extraordinary amount, the Weather Bureau's reports indicate that this storm followed a month of unsettled weather patterns that alternated between freezes and thaws and a high amount of precipitation. Furthermore, an unusually high amount of precipitation had occurred in January 1913. The ground was saturated when the March storm arrived. According to the Weather Bureau's local office, the flooding that resulted "cost the lives of scores of people, rendered many thousands homeless, and destroyed property beyond estimate." The bureau director explained, "The enormous losses over such an extended area is unprecedented in the history of this portion of the United States, and it must follow that an occurrence so unusual must have been produced by extraordinary weather conditions."[1] Although extreme weather clearly contributed to this disaster, many other factors exacerbated the effects of the weather event. Indiana history illuminates the story of the 1913 flood, which

Colton's Map of Indiana, circa 1886. *Indiana Historical Society.*

became known as the "Great Flood," and it was the event against which future floods were compared.

The disaster revealed an interdependent—yet conflicted—relationship between the people and the landscape of Indiana. By the early twentieth century, Indianapolis and urban centers across the state boasted their growing factories, employed residents and plentiful homes. Yet the concentration of homes and businesses in floodplains, along with the accumulation of human waste and industrial pollution in rivers, made the effects of the flood much worse. By 1913, development had progressed to the point where residents were faced with a philosophical dilemma concerning the value and wisdom of continuing to encroach on and manipulate the flood-prone landscape. The apparent effects of past actions raised questions about how to proceed.

Although the 1913 flood caught the attention of Hoosiers, the immediate concern was recovery. Governor Samuel M. Ralston and President Woodrow Wilson rushed to the assistance of communities, while mayors organized efforts to provide aid to flood sufferers. Business owners tried to salvage what they could to help others. Church groups, charitable organizations and neighbors pitched in to help families clean up, disinfect, repair their homes and restart their lives. Citizens, city administrators and policy makers soon turned to debates about what could be done to prevent a future flood like this one.

Today, towns display plaques and lines on the sides of buildings to mark the height of the 1913 floodwaters. Archives hold photographs and newspaper clippings about the disaster. The Great Flood lives in the memories of Hoosiers in these ways, but in other ways, it has been erased. Many towns have significantly changed in the last one hundred years, and the flood changed the trajectory of some when businesses did not survive or when they decided to move to another location. When we view black-and-white photographs of the Great Flood, it may seem like the distant past, but its story remains relevant today. The flood not only provides insight into a location's history but also its present.

This book shares the experiences and responses of the people of Indiana when the 1913 disaster occurred. It also uncovers the state's history that helps explain the events of the spring of 1913. It seeks to answer questions of what made this flood "great," how it became "great" and what it signified for the future.

1.

THE LANDSCAPE OF INDIANA

Interconnectedness is the sinister companion of chaos.
—Terry G. Jordan, geographer, "The Concept and Method"

WATER AND THE STATE

Indiana has a number of natural water sources, from the winding Ohio River shaping its southern border to Lake Michigan carving out its northwestern border. In between, the state encompasses numerous rivers, streams, lakes, ponds and swamps. The Wabash River—which has cultural importance in the state's song, in literature and in nomenclature—rises in Ohio thirty miles east of the Indiana border, then stretches in a westerly direction across the northern portion of Indiana through the cities of Bluffton, Wabash and Peru before it veers southwesterly toward Lafayette. From there, the river flows through Covington and Terre Haute before creating the border between the states of Illinois and Indiana, and then, it joins the Ohio River at the confluence in the states of Indiana, Illinois and Kentucky.[2] Some of its larger tributaries include the Little Wabash, Embarrass, White, Tippecanoe, Eel, Salamonie and Mississinewa Rivers. The Wabash River Basin includes thirty-three thousand square miles, covering 68 percent of the state.

This interconnected web of water across and around the state often caused chaos when early settlers tried to navigate the geography and later developers tried to manage it. Apart from the Ohio River and Lake

Michigan at its borders, the state's waters are not commercially navigable. This separation and exclusion from surrounding commercial markets caused a lot of consternation for state boosters. Although the Wabash River Basin connected a large swath of the state, it did not provide easy access to the Great Lakes. This shortcoming prompted state officials to plan for the Wabash and Erie Canal, which would provide a connecting route from Lake Erie to the Ohio River. Its construction began near Fort Wayne in 1832, after the project experienced delays in obtaining land grants and employing the necessary engineers and thousands of Irish immigrant workers. The project was expanded after a short section of the canal between Fort Wayne and Huntington was completed and Indiana Governor Noah Noble signed the Mammoth Internal Improvements Act of 1836. The act not only called for "alteration of Indiana's drainage system with canals, locks, aqueducts, and dams to make the major river systems navigable and provide outlets to Lake Michigan and Lake Erie," but it also called for significant bond debt.[3]

The scheme, as it was often called, was financed by a $10 million loan, which bankrupted the state after the economic panic of 1837. As former Purdue University English professor Paul Fatout put it, the plan was "conceived in madness and nourished by delusion."[4] The interest on the borrowed money alone amounted to ten times the state's revenues from taxes, and by 1841, state officials admitted that Indiana could not make the interest payments (let alone repay the principal). Indiana historian Peter Harstad wrote, "Men and money succumbed to the environment… [and] the resulting political and fiscal embarrassment affected Indiana permanently."[5] Indeed, this experience led Indiana legislators to change the constitution in 1851 to prohibit the state from contracting debt except in limited circumstances, such as to provide public defense. The state did extend the Wabash and Erie Canal as far as Evansville in 1853, "making it the longest canal in the country." Although the "southern section was often inoperable and never attracted much traffic," the section northeast of Terre Haute provided an "important gateway for shipping agriculture products to northeastern markets."[6]

Swampland presented another obstacle to settlers and boosters who wanted to make "productive" use of the young state's land. The 1787 Northwest Ordinance had created a territory, opening the door for westward expansion and the formation of the future states of Indiana, Ohio, Michigan, Illinois and Wisconsin. The percentage of swampland that eventually became Indiana is difficult to ascertain, but a study of pre-settlement land surveyors' records and soil survey maps indicate that, in

2,000 LABORERS

WANTED

ON THE CENTRAL

CANAL

Of Indiana.

THE great Central Canal of Indiana is intended to connect the waters of Lake Erie and the Ohio river, and will be about 400 miles in length. In addition to that part already completed and under contract in the middle and northern part of the state, TWENTY miles commencing at Evansville, on the Ohio river, its southern termination, and extending into the interior, were put under contract in November last; since which time the work has been steadily progressing.

No section of country holds out greater inducements to the industrious laborer than the state of Indiana, and particularly that portion of it contiguous to the Central Canal, from the fact that there is much of the land belonging to the general government remaining unentered, which may be purchased at one dollar and twenty-five cents per acre; affording to those who are desirous of doing so, an opportunity of securing to themselves, with the avails of a few months' labor, a permanent home in this flourishing and rapidly growing state.

The contractors are now paying $20 per month, and the fare and lodgings furnished, is of the most comfortable character. It may not be amiss to say that the acting commissioner reserves, by an express provision in all contracts, the right to see that every laborer receives his just dues; therefore, no man need lose one dollar of his wages, if he pursues a proper course.

It is probable that more of this Canal will be put under contract during the coming fall or spring, when an opportunity will be offered to those who show themselves qualified of proposing for work.

Laborers coming from the south can take passage to Evansville, and find immediate employment upon their arrival. By order of JOHN A. GRAHAM, *Act. Com.*
Canal Office, Evansville, May 1, 1837. C. G. VOORHIES, *Res'dt Eng.*

EVANSVILLE JOURNAL Power.

Advertisement for laborers on the Indiana Central Canal, *Evansville Journal*, 1837. *Bass Photo Co. Collection, Indiana Historical Society.*

1820, swamps, wetlands and floodplain forests were abundant. For counties in the northwestern quarter of the state, comprising 3,224,121 acres, 50 percent of the land was either permanently ponded or seasonally ponded wetland. That percentage does not include acreage that was simply plagued with drainage problems. While this information is available for certain counties, surveyor records and soil survey maps are not available for many other counties.[7] From the Kankakee Swamp in northwestern Indiana (known as the "Everglades of the North"), to the state's northeastern counties, Indianapolis and the state's southwestern corner, the land was undeniably swampy.

Evidence of the state's landscape history also comes from legislative and civic records. In 1850, the federal government adopted the Swamp Lands Act. The westward movement in America promoted land acquisition, and draining wetlands was one scheme the federal government implemented to accomplish this goal. Indiana settlers and developers, along with people in other states, took full advantage of this law. The desire to control flooding and reclaim barren wastelands overrode larger thinking about the possible long-term impacts that might have occurred, especially downstream from drained swamps. In 1853, the state committee on swamplands submitted its report to the Indiana senate, referring to the "desolate waste" of Indiana that could be transformed into a "habitat for industrious, healthy, and happy people."[8] Environmental historian Ann Vileisis explained that the destruction of wetlands began with the cultural disdain for swamps, coupled with the recognition that wealth could be extracted from wetland properties.[9] The words from the state committee expressed a desire for the advancement of society, not the misuse of valuable wetlands, and one could say that Indiana's settlers believed they were improving the land from its natural state of wastefulness and ridding it of breeding grounds for mosquito-borne diseases. As historian Stephen F. Strausberg argued, the lack of expertise and corruption involved with implementation of the Swamp Lands Act in Indiana told another story and reflected the impact of local culture on the environment.[10] Indiana, unlike other states, decided to retain title to its swamplands, selling acreage to settlers with the understanding that the state would drain the land in the future. Due to a number of unforeseen events, including corruption at the local level, the state broke that promise.[11] The Swamp Lands Act did, however, set in motion actions that converted Indiana's wetlands into towns and farmland that were vulnerable to future flooding.

The landscape and glacial history of Indiana challenged those who were wishing to improve its profitability. Following the success of draining Beaver Lake in Newton County, engineers and entrepreneurs believed they could drain the Kankakee Swamp. The Kankakee Valley Draining Company, along with a number of other ditch-digging enterprises, intended to reengineer the landscape. The Kankakee River wound 240 miles, with an estimated two thousand bends from its source near South Bend, Indiana, and westward through seven Indiana counties, and it had an average fall per mile of less than four inches until it crossed the state line near Momence, Illinois. The plan for improving the river included "constructing a better main channel… straightening and deepening" the streams that emptied into the river and "digging a large number of lateral ditches through the swamps to the improved channels." This plan of "judicious drainage" would claim at least 400,000 acres from the marsh. Along with marshes, swamps and quicksand, engineers encountered a one-and-a-half-mile-long limestone ledge called the Momence Ledge that stood in the way of efforts to drain the Kankakee Swamp. In 1883, the state's chief engineer reported to Governor Albert G. Porter that, once the river had been straightened, its velocity would increase and carry with it "large quantities of soil and sand," making the removal of the ledge "a necessity for the proper improvement of the river."[12] The state engineer proposed blasting an opening through the rocky ledge. Unfortunately, the ledge was located twelve miles west of the Indiana border in Momence, Illinois. As state boosters saw it, below the ledge, Illinois benefited from a lush, productive valley, while above the ledge, Indiana suffered from unproductive, marshy wasteland. Following years of political controversies, litigation and debate, state engineers excavated a width of three hundred feet and a mean depth of over two feet from the limestone ledge to help reclaim the marsh. Manipulating the Kankakee River to do their bidding was next on their list, and the river was straightened to the Indiana-Illinois state line by 1917. Despite their efforts, expertise and money spent, the marshy landscape refused to become well-drained land for farming and development purposes.[13]

In the late nineteenth and early twentieth centuries, many engineers, landowners and government officials supported massive and costly efforts to manipulate the existing landscape into what was, in their opinion, a more beautiful and richer place. The chief engineer's 1883 report to the governor made similar proposals for draining marshland in Allen and Huntington Counties in northeastern Indiana, which also involved the removal of a limestone ledge that obstructed the drainage of Little River. The Cypress Swamp in Knox County in the southwestern corner of the state also needed attention in order to reclaim and improve the value of that land. And a ditch that had previously been dug to drain the Dechee River also needed to be improved.[14]

These schemes and engineering feats offer many lessons about Indiana's past and present landscape, and the actions that were taken by settlers of European descent to control, manipulate and change the landscape they

Dredge on the Kankakee River, Burrows Camp, Porter County, 1909. *Steven R. Shook Collection.*

encountered sheds light on the environmental implications for future Indiana residents. Viewing the landscape of Indiana as "history" reveals a changing geography—one in which inhabitants cut down hardwood forests, extracted natural gas, mined coal, quarried limestone, drained swamps, dug ditches, filled in ravines, built levees, rerouted rivers, dug canals and constructed bridges, roads and railroads.[15] Hoosiers maintained a relationship with Indiana's natural resources that was rooted in continuously changing the landscape to meet their needs.

The relationship between Hoosiers and the rivers in their towns has been one of conflict and misunderstanding—people did not appreciate their interdependence with their rivers. They did not respect the river's nature and cycles. They did not acknowledge that expansion into the floodplains, along with building levees and bridges, would increase the devastation they experienced from flooding. They did not understand that dumping their waste into the river would cause health problems. Certainly, in the nineteenth century, most people did not understand the concept of ecological systems. Although early settlers quickly learned that flooding along the state's waterways would frequently occur, they accepted that challenge and clung to the many advantages of the region.

LOCATING THE CAPITAL CITY

Indianapolis was the state's third capital city, following Vincennes and Corydon. Both Vincennes and Corydon are in the hilly southern portion of the original territory, near the Wabash and Ohio Rivers, respectively. With statehood in 1816, the Indiana general assembly sought a more central location for the capital. The commissioners tasked with finding the ideal location came from southern Indiana, where the land was knobby and intricately laced with streams. The prospect of building a town on land "as level as a barn floor" was appealing to them.[16] The commissioners chose the future site of Indianapolis because it was a central location in the state, it had level and rich soil for farming and they believed White River was navigable. White River soon proved to be non-navigable for commercial traffic. The commissioners also failed to give due consideration to the issue of drainage. In their defense, the commissioners visited the site in 1820, which was apparently a dry year. The following year revealed the more common, wet conditions of Indianapolis.

A young Catharine Merrill noted in her diary that she heard some men tell her father, Samuel Merrill, the future of Indianapolis looked bleak. As she recounted their discussion, the place was "situated in a vast mud-hole, which could never be dried up so as to be depended upon." Along with White River and Fall Creek, which regularly overflowed their banks, she described Pogue's Run as a bayou that "spread out over everything," which was "mostly made up of mud, and mud drowns worse than water, as," she continued, "Mr. Norwood's cow could prove if it were alive."[17]

Geologists have conjectured that the site where Indianapolis now stands was in some past age the bed of a lake. The city's average elevation is about 720 feet above sea level, but it has somewhat higher ground on all sides. Pogue's Run, a swampy valley, ran diagonally across the site. An extensive swamp called Fletcher's Swamp stretched across the northeast portion of the city's original Mile Square and, in wet seasons, discharged its overflow through the site via ravines. During floods, Fall Creek emptied its surplus water through Fletcher's Swamp and the same ravines. A number of deep places developed where water stood for most of the year, and water puddled for weeks during the wet seasons in low places scattered through the dense forest. In the area that later became West Indianapolis, just southwest of Greenlawn Cemetery, there was a body of stagnant water called "Graveyard Pond" that was covered by a green, filthy scum and inhabited by snakes and frogs in the summer. Lake McCarty laid in

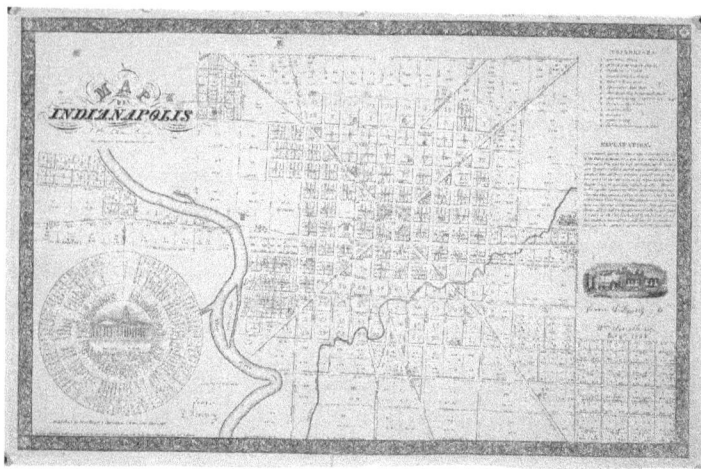

Sullivan map of Indianapolis, circa 1836, showing White River and Pogue's Run. *Indiana Historical Society.*

the low ground between Ray and Morris Streets; it was both a natural and manmade pond, as its size and depth increased due to excavations and fills for the National Road. Settlers in the area maintained that it rained much more in Indianapolis in the city's early years than it did later, which is probable since the conditions were "peculiarly favorable to local evaporation and reprecipitation" at that time.[18]

The muddy location meant unhealthy conditions for the settlers. Unfortunately, as the secretary of the Indiana State Board of Health John N. Hurty noted in 1908, "Almost nothing was known of the disease-bearing possibilities of water," and early settlers considered diarrhea, dysentery and typhoid "among the necessary concomitants of life."[19] The diseases that were common in Indianapolis included cholera, consumption, scarlatina, diphtheria, dysentery, pneumonia, influenza, typhoid, cerebro-spinal meningitis and tuberculosis. The common diseases shifted over time, but without the bacterial key, doctors found it difficult to distinguish between the various maladies and often categorized them simply as miasma and epizootic.[20] It was not until the mosquito theory arrived on the scene, around 1898, that people understood the cause of malaria, one of the more common diseases. Until then (and likely even after), people thought malaria was the product of the miasma rising from the damp soil

Indiana State Board of Health Tuberculosis Group, circa 1910. *Indiana Historical Society, M0384.*

and decaying vegetation—or possibly the alternations of heat and cold. Most of the early settlers "served a regular apprenticeship at the ague," including the doctors who treated them.[21] They did recognize that the disease became less common as the land was cleared—another reason to take control of the topography.

Along with health concerns, the environment often created social, political and economic upheaval. During floods, the ravines became raging torrents. Before Washington Street was graded for the National Road, the ravine that crossed Washington Street was a broad valley, and it was so deep that, in flood time, the water "would swim a horse" (a frequently used Hoosierism for measuring the depth of water). The city almost became an island in flood times; it was surrounded by ravines, swamps and creeks. In the early years of settlement, the floods did little damage because the area's population was small and cabins were constructed out of harm's way, but they obstructed travel. The April and May 1821 publications of the *Gazette* were suspended because the editors had gone out of town and could not get back through the floods. On May 10, 1824, the *Western Censor* printed an apology for its limited outside news because the mail carriers were not able to get into or out of town. In March and April 1826, the mail deliveries were stopped for several days due to flooding.[22]

By the flood of 1828, greater damage occurred because farmers had begun to cultivate the bottomlands. Floodwaters washed away fences and covered fertile fields with sand and gravel. Property owners began building earthen levees to protect their land from floodwaters, but the levees narrowed the current of floodwaters, especially those that were built by riverbank property owners.[23] When engineers designed bridges to cross the river, they were too short, and the bridges acted like dams during times of high water, restricting the flow of water and increasing its intensity.

As the settlement of Indianapolis progressed, people encroached more and more on the existing environment of the site. The Indiana legislature passed an act on February 4, 1837, appointing a commission to oversee the drainage of the swamps and lowlands northeast of the Mile Square of Indianapolis. The legislators decided to cut a state ditch. The ditch disposed of the trouble with the ravines for about ten years until the banks gave way on New Year's Day in 1847. As described by Indianapolis historian Jacob Piatt Dunn, "[The] water came down its old channels in volume that startled those who had invaded them." According to one report:

> *Israel Jennings, who had been living peacefully at the northwest corner of Walnut and New Jersey Streets, was awakened by a noise in the night, and on rising from his high-post bed to investigate went into water almost to his waist. He managed to get ashore with his family; and in the morning, rescued his belongings by aid of a wagon and team. The flood of 1847 was quite general throughout the state and did so much damage that the legislature provided for the re-appraisement of real property that had been injured, and for change of the tax duplicates to the extent of the injury.*[24]

The ditch was repaired, but it broke again in June 1858, and the waters again found their old channels. After another set of repairs to the ditch, it seemed to be fixed for good.

People forgot about the ravines. But on June 1, 1875, a severe electrical and windstorm, followed by a deluge of rain, visited the city. This time, the waters surged through the fashionable residential district of the city, flooding the first floors of the homes in the vicinity of Twelfth Street and Pennsylvania Avenue. After 1875, the ravines were filled in so that the trace of their course was barely visible, except in the occasional slope of street grades and lots. Some people believed that the course of the filled ravines was traceable by "typhoid belts" along their old channels and tributary swales. Medical professionals did not attach much importance to this belief, but they did believe the old ravines affected wells, which were commonly sunk only to the first level. In 1887, Dr. Samuel E. Earp, the first city sanitarian, noted that he did not consider the city's water supply good because it was drawn from a swampy source.[25]

GROWTH AND MODERNITY

Until the arrival of the first railroad in Indianapolis in 1847, the flood-prone land south of Pogue's Run was of little importance to the city. Between 1860 and 1870, however, the city started expanding in that direction as a result of the new railroad system, and city developers turned their attentions to this troublesome area. Lake McCarty was one of the natural features causing problems; the "Virginia River" was another. In 1866, the Indianapolis Common Council ordered Nicholas McCarty Jr. to cut a ditch through his land to drain the pond into White River. In 1868, the common council adopted a more permanent solution by levying a sewer tax of fifteen cents on every one hundred dollars of property value and appropriating funds to build a sewer through Ray Street to drain Lake McCarty into White River. The ordinance also authorized McCarty to fill in the pond once it was drained.[26]

Likewise, city officials focused their attentions on Virginia River. The Indianapolis Committee on Sewers classified this "so-called river" as a mere stream with its two-mile winding course through the city. After heavy rains, however, it transformed into a swiftly flowing river that ranged from fifteen to one hundred feet wide and ran deep enough in places to "swim a horse." As the city grew, the river became obstructed by street grades and culverts. The river started forming deep ponds along its course, and its channel was deep and rapid, carrying a formidable body of water after heavy rains. The committee on sewers noted in its 1869 report that the Virginia River had cost the city "many thousands of dollars in culverts and embankments, and there [had] also been large sums claimed as damages from its overflow." Noting further that these evils would increase with future street improvements, the committee wanted to construct another sewer line. Instead, the common council approved lodging the river in the South Street and Kentucky Avenue sewer.[27] With that, the river was removed from sight and mind.

The city continually took steps to conquer its drainage and flooding problems, and in the process, the rivers, streams and surrounding landscape underwent dramatic changes. As the town of Indianapolis grew and progressed, additional concerns rose to the surface. Garbage and human waste disposal became an important problem that, when combined with drainage and flooding problems, had to be addressed by city administrators.

While Indianapolis developed into a modern city, its citizens found alternative uses for the non-navigable White River. These changes, which were made in the name of progress and improvement, held serious ramifications for both the river and the city's residents. For example, in the late nineteenth century, sanitary engineers designed the growing city's sewer system in the customary method so that waste flowed into the river. Moreover, with its location on the National Road—at the "crossroads of America"—Indianapolis developed into a center for railroads, stockyards and industry. Property owners believed that the swampland close to White River was most profitable when it was devoted to these endeavors, resulting in overdevelopment and consumption of the fragile floodplain and treatment of the river as a waste receptacle. Simultaneous with growth in Indianapolis, agriculture and industry expanded up and down the river, with the river receiving the brunt of runoff and discharge from flourishing towns, businesses and farms.

Despite early uncertainties, state legislators had established Indianapolis as the capital city, and state boosters and settlers forged ahead with that decision, adopting a mindset of conquering this new frontier. They drained swamps, covered rivers and filled ravines. The founders also set the stage for the environmental future of the city—an environment in which flooding would become increasingly more severe, costly and unhealthy. Consequently, the relationship between the city's residents and the landscape progressed into one of distrust and disrespect. People knew flooding could occur but did not exactly know when. In fact, residents enjoyed years without flooding, making it possible to temporarily forget about drainage and flooding problems. They also believed that the actions that were taken to conquer the landscape would successfully prevent future flooding.

Although the capital city provides a large-scale example of the environmental impact of growth and development, similar processes occurred in cities and towns across the state in the nineteenth and early twentieth centuries. The 1913 flood is referred to as the Great Flood in part because it impacted a large portion of the country and because of the storm's intensity. Its greatness also derived from its arrival at a time when people had settled in, grown roots, built homes and civic structures and invested in municipal infrastructure.[28]

By 1913, the character of Indiana's landscape and waterways had withstood almost a century of development. Many of those efforts had been aimed at draining the land not only for development, but also for flood prevention. Yet Indiana's residents had experienced floods that were increasingly more damaging. Apart from the loss of lives and the threat to the residents' health and livelihoods, the monetary costs of floods had been great. The Indiana State Planning Board prepared a report estimating the costs of major floods in Indiana's history, as shown in chart 1. In the chart, which was prepared following the 1937 devastating flood, the board noted that the monetary damages from earlier floods were fewer, and it highlighted the connection between land use—that investment in physical improvements—and the damage resulting from flooding.[29] As noted by geographers and environmental historians, people are connected to and a part of nature, meaning that efforts to control, manipulate and make sense of nature often affect people in unexpected ways. A flood disaster cannot be taken out of context; acknowledging interconnectedness is important to understanding the chaos.[30] In this case, the history of settlement and urban growth sheds light on what happened during the Great Flood of 1913.

CHART 1

FLOOD DAMAGES IN INDIANA

February 1832	$2,000,000
February 1847	$2,000,000
August 1875	$10,000,000
February 1883	$5,000,000
February 1884	$10,000,000
March 1904	$3,000,000
January 1907	$1,000,000
March 1913	$25,000,000
January 1937	$50,000,000

Courtesy of Dennis O'Harrow, State Planning Board of Indiana, "Indiana Flood Damage," February 1937.

2.

THE GREAT FLOOD OF 1913

It is but the irony of Nature that, when her natural order is altered, she objects.
—Archibald Shaw (1915)

In the middle of March 1913, severe storms blew across the country from the northwest. Local newspapers reported tornados, floods and fire from Nebraska to Illinois as the storms slowly marched toward Indiana. Reports of deaths, destroyed homes, ravaged railroad tracks and bridges, downed telephone lines and stranded communities filled the front pages. The *Indianapolis News* reported the destructive path of the storms with flood reports from every city in the state located near a river. Articles titled "$500,000 Loss at Peru," "Over the Muncie Levee," "Boats in Carmel Streets," "Danville Cars Stopped," "Bloomington Is Cut Off" and "Shelbyville Levee Breaks" appeared on just one page of the March 25 edition of the *Indianapolis News*. As an aid to follow the story of the Great Flood, see chart 2 with the two-week 1913 calendar of dates during which the storm, rising waters and devastation moved across the state.

Indiana residents are no strangers to rain or windstorms, but the storms that began on Easter Sunday, March 23, 1913, delivered a destructive weather event that would break records and leave lasting memories for those who lived through it. Due to high-pressure systems from Canada in the north and from Bermuda in the south, a low pressure system condensed into a long trough that connected them both and then stalled over the Ohio Valley. The blended storm overflowed tributaries and their drainage areas both north

CHART 2

TWO-WEEK 1913 REFERENCE CALENDAR
FOR INDIANA'S GREAT FLOOD

Sunday (Easter)	March 23
Monday	March 24
Tuesday	March 25
Wednesday	March 26
Thursday	March 27
Friday	March 28
Saturday	March 29
Sunday	March 30
Monday	March 31
Tuesday	April 1
Wednesday	April 2
Thursday	April 3
Friday	April 4
Saturday	April 5

and south of the Ohio River. As described in a study that was conducted for Indiana University in 1915, "At no time in the history of the Ohio Valley had so much rain fallen in a 72-hour period" as fell in the five days from March 23 to March 27. Although many local areas had received the same amount of rain in the past, the study's authors explained that "never [had] there been such a heavy rainfall over so large an area in so short a time." The ground was not frozen, and there was not any melting ice or snow that contributed to the accumulating water. However, the ground was already saturated from earlier rainfall before this storm arrived. See chart 3, which shows the rainfall amounts that were reported from weather stations across the state.[31]

When answering the question of why the 1913 flood was called the "Great Flood," we can point to the combination of weather patterns and existing conditions. The extreme weather event is only one part of the story. Additional contributing factors also came into play, including the particular environmental history and circumstances of each place. When hearing the stories of places impacted by the Great Flood, it is important to note their location in relation to rivers, creeks and swamps, their past experiences with flooding and their settlement and development history. What follows are, first,

CHART 3
RAINFALL TOTALS REPORTED FROM INDIANA WEATHER STATIONS,
MARCH 23–27, 1913 (LISTED ALPHABETICALLY)

Station	Rainfall in Inches	Station	Rainfall in Inches
Anderson	6.99	Laporte	1.65
Auburn	5.39	Marion	8.08
Berne	7.31	Mauzy	9.65
Bloomington	9.20	Moores Hill	6.29
Bluffton	7.50	Mt. Vernon	4.78
Butlerville	9.27	Paoli	7.52
Cambridge City	9.38	Plymouth	4.22
Collegeville	4.44	Princeton	7.35
Columbus	9.92	Richmond	11.15
Connersville	9.98	Rochester	5.76
Crawfordsville	8.00	Rockville	7.02
Delphi	5.96	Rome	5.78
Elliston	7.59	Salamonia	9.04
Eminence	5.25	Scottsburg	7.77
Evansville	5.52	Seymour	8.05
Farmland	8.94	Shelbyville	7.11
Fort Wayne	5.36	Shoals	9.06
French Lick	9.87	South Bend	3.34
Greenfield	7.28	Terre Haute	4.56
Hammond	2.99	Vandersburg	6.78
Hickory Hill	7.35	Vevay	7.45
Huntingburg	7.29	Vincennes	9.40
Indianapolis	6.01	Washington	8.97
Jeffersonville	5.77	Whitestown	7.05
Judyville	5.02	Whitney	1.87
Knox	4.14	Winona Lake	4.76
Kokomo	6.10	Worthington	10.13
Lafayette	5.27		

Courtesy of Hal P. Bybee and Clyde A. Malott, "The Flood of 1913 in the Lower White River Region of Indiana," Indiana University Studies: Contribution to Knowledge Made by Instructors and Advanced Students of the University *2, no. 22 (October 1914): 126–27, www.babel.hathitrust.org*

a brief history of several cities from across the state and their experiences during the 1913 flood. Second, the effects of the flood in many other Indiana cities and towns are briefly recounted. The flood brought similar devastation to these places, and yet, each story is different and noteworthy.

THE STORM CROSSES THE STATE LINE

The storm entered the state near Terre Haute on the evening of Easter Sunday, March 23. Sitting on high land, as its name reflects, the city's residents did not expect a major flood. The Terre Haute Town Company had purchased land situated on the Wabash River from Joseph Kitchell on September 13, 1816. William Hoggatt, a surveyor and engineer employed by the town company, selected the site because, as he explained, it was a beautiful place for a town, with the river running straight and the land high and rising from the river. The name Terre Haute had been given to this place a hundred years before, and it had been a natural gathering place for a Native American village, a trading post and a military fort. Historian H.C. Bradsby described it as a place "where nature and man were so completely in accord as to the future of the place" with the Wabash River at their feet, a "natural artery" playing the role of "the world's greatest civilizer." When Vigo County was created two years later, Terre Haute gained the position of county seat despite its sparse settlement and trials with malaria.[32]

With financing from the town company, its status as county seat and its prime riverine location, Terre Haute soon became a thriving city. Despite the city center's position on high ground, the surrounding land had less favorable qualities. When constructing the National Road to Terre Haute in the 1830s, workers had battled "seas of impassable mud and mire" and built grades to cross the "swampy and boggy" places. As the city grew and attracted more businesses and residents, it spread beyond that high ground and spurred adjacent settlements. When the Wabash and Erie Canal reached the town in 1850, the population had grown to 3,572. By 1890, the thriving city's population exceeded 31,000.[33]

The city's history of growth and development into a modern city affected the impact of the 1913 storm. Ushered in with a tornado that blew through the area, the storm killed 17 people, injured another 150, demolished homes and razed businesses. With the heavy rain following the tornado, the Wabash River rose rapidly and overflowed its banks, toppling homes in West Terre Haute and destroying the village of Taylorville (on the west side of the river).

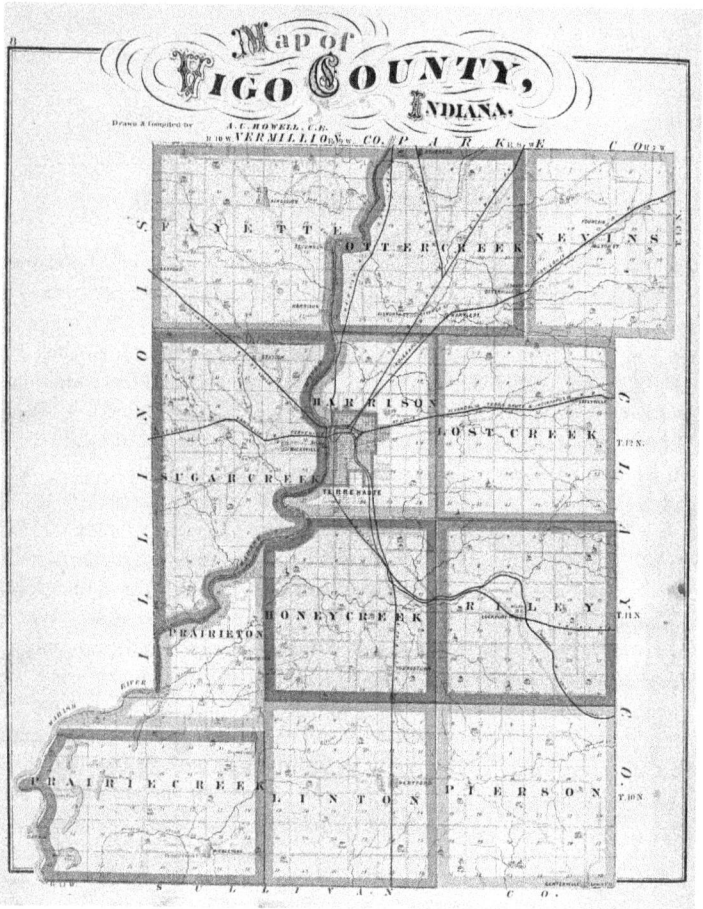

Map of Vigo County, circa 1874, showing the location of Terre Haute and waterways.
Indiana Historical Society.

On Monday, descriptions of the flood conditions noted, "Another flood is eminent in the lower Wabash Valley....Lowlands, both north and south of the city, are already flooded." Sugar Creek had flooded the river bottoms south of the levee, and a levee broke near the creek, inundating West Terre Haute and prompting families to flee their homes. The National Road was covered with water and was impassable for almost a mile. Water from Clear Creek also "stretched over a large territory." Despite the familiar refrain of flooding in low-lying areas, some of the oldest residents said they had not seen the Wabash River rise as rapidly as it did at this time.[34]

On Wednesday of that week, the Wabash River was continuing to rise by four inches an hour, and the highwater mark had reached twenty-eight feet. With hundreds of houses surrounded by water, families abandoned their homes and possessions in the hopes of saving their own lives. Despite the city's position on higher ground and sandbag embankments, water swept into the city and seeped through the walls of the power plant. Police guarded the wagon bridge and railroad structures as fears grew that they would give way to the rushing water. Meanwhile, fifty men moved two switch engines and four flat cars onto the west end of the Big Four Bridge to try to stabilize it and prevent a washout. The floodwaters forced the owners of the Vigo Clay and American Clay Companies to close, putting two hundred men out of work, and another five thousand miners found themselves unemployed when all the mines in the area closed due to the threat of flooding. The Valentine Meat Packing House faced imminent flooding, and some of the stock (mostly hogs) had to be moved to the upper deck of the building. George Davis's grocery store at Fifth Street and Maple Avenue had been carried off its foundation and was "floating around." Terre Haute was "rapidly becoming shut off from the world" as railroad lines were closed from track washouts and communication lines failed. These were just a few reports of the conditions that Wednesday.[35]

The Wabash River crested at 33.25 feet on Thursday.[36] Three feet of water in the plant forced the manager of Citizens Gas & Fuel Company to close, leaving the city in darkness for the night, and he cautioned that the resumption of operations that Friday depended on the river. The Vandalia and Big Four railroad beds washed away from the force of water for nearly a mile west of the river, and reports arrived saying that the Chicago & Eastern Illinois bridge at Clinton and the Hillsdale wagon bridge had both been swept away. Police answered pleas from West Terre Haute for boat rescues, fire destroyed Fort Heyden and the raging river nearly claimed the lives of two of the firemen. Railroad passengers sat in cars that were stranded on the tracks in Terre Haute, and nine hundred head of cattle stood in fifteen inches of water waiting for their rescue. Terre Hauteans received news that the levees, including the Brevoort and Hutsonville levees and "every large levee" between Terre Haute and Mount Carmel, Illinois, which had withstood earlier floods in 1875, 1883 and 1897, had not lasted this storm.[37]

Flooding on North Sixth Street near Collet Park in Terre Haute, circa 1913. *Vigo County Historical Society.*

West Terre Haute Flood
Mch. 27. 1913

Lee Ave.   Photo by *Austin Hamilton Fake*

Flooding in West Terre Haute on Lee Avenue, circa 1913. *Vigo County Historical Society.*

On Friday, the river level slowly began to fall at a half inch an hour, but by then, the catastrophe had made a lasting impact. The floodwaters had claimed the lives of four people, in addition to the seventeen lives that had been lost in the initial tornado. While "rows of homes [stood] in the middle of the pond with the waves lapping against the upper gables," others had

The flooded Clinton Railroad Line in northern Terre Haute during the 1913 flood. *Vigo County Historical Society.*

A flood scene on the Wabash in Terre Haute, circa 1913. *Lambert M. Christie Postcard Album, Indiana Historical Society, P0326.*

been washed away, but others on higher ground had escaped the damage. Regardless of each person's story, the entire community and surrounding area would long remember the havoc wrought by this flood. But the storm did not languish in Terre Haute; it continued on a path of destruction across the state.[38]

PERU: THE MOST DESOLATED CITY

Peru, which is 114 miles northeast of Terre Haute and also on the Wabash River, suffered severe flooding in March 1913. William N. Hood founded Peru in 1834 with promises that the city would serve as the seat of Miami County, as it had all the advantages of being located on the Wabash and Erie Canal. The Wabash River geographically divided the northern and southern portions of the city, and the Wabash and Mississinewa Rivers met at the city's southeastern corner. The city's future success seemed assured given its ideal location. The stretch of canal linking Fort Wayne to Peru was completed in time for a grand celebration on July 4, 1837. The crowds that gathered along the banks were disappointed when the boats did not arrive; as reported in the *Peru Forester*, the canal banks had "absorbed the water much faster than was anticipated." Later trips to Peru were successful, and the canal did bring growth and prosperity to the area for a while. Although the canal project bankrupted the state by 1839 and the state's expanding network of rail lines rapidly surpassed the usefulness of the canal, it had served its purpose in establishing Peru as a vibrant and important community. Thus, the city's early relationship with these waterways and development around them contributed to devastating flood events in its future.[39]

The 1847 flood was the first major flood on record to occur in the city, but it was just the first. Miami County historian Arthur L. Bodurtha described the debate that arose among residents about whether or not the 1883 floodwater levels had exceeded those of the 1847 flood. As the 1847 flood height had been marked on an elm tree near the river, some young men took a rowboat and a lantern out on the night that the 1883 flood was at its highest to inspect the tree. They claimed that the 1847 mark was below the water; however, the next morning, ice rings hanging on the tree were about three inches below the 1847 mark. Regardless, both floods, along with other interim and later floods, caused significant and repeated damage to residents' homes and businesses and the city's industries and infrastructure. Although railroads were preferred by this time, the 1875 flood washed away a portion

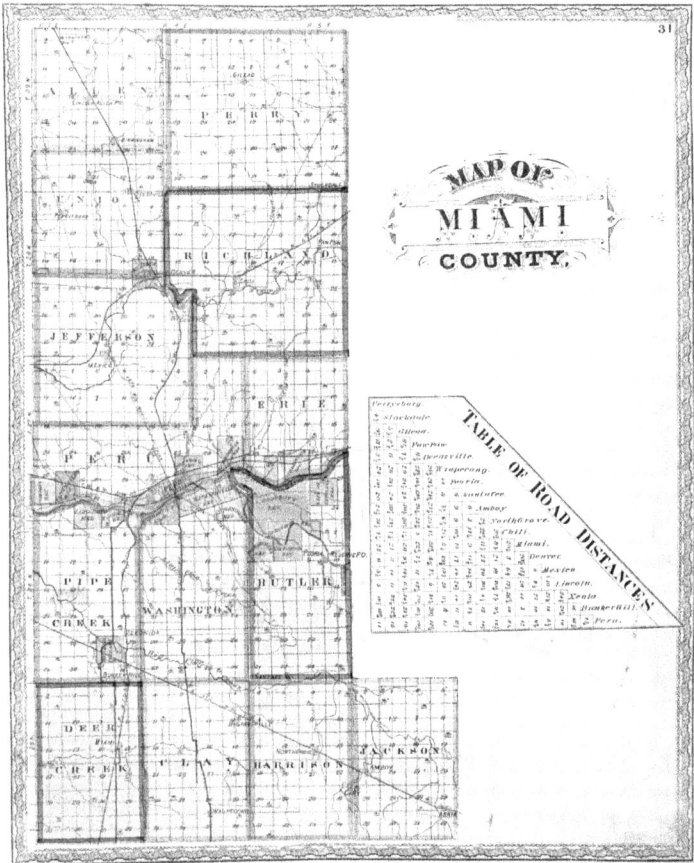

A map of Miami County, circa 1877, showing the location of Peru and waterways. *Indiana Historical Society.*

of the canal on the east side of Peru, sealing its demise as a commercially viable mode of transportation. With little funds available for repairs, the once-promising canal and the stranded boats were left to decay.[40]

Although Peru's residents had previously experienced floods, the 1913 flood broke earlier records and caused more damage. The Wabash River extended much farther from its banks, and a tree on the bank of the river no longer sufficed as a marker for its possible heights. All future floods were then measured by a mark on the side of a building in downtown Peru. In 1913, the rain arrived on Easter Sunday and continued for three days. By Monday evening, fire alarm whistles sounded to warn residents that the Wabash River had left its banks. By midnight, the river flooded the electric light station, and the city was left in darkness. On Tuesday, both the Wabash and Mississinewa Rivers had submerged south Peru. The floodwaters crested in the early morning hours on Wednesday, and by then, both south and north Peru had been flooded except for a few high points. Peruvians were surrounded by water and disconnected from the outside world as the Broadway Street bridge and Union Traction Company bridge had collapsed, railroad trains could not reach the city, interurban cars were stranded, only one telephone line was open to Indianapolis and only one Western Union telegraph wire was open to Chicago.[41]

During the evening of Tuesday, March 25, Governor Ralston received a telegraph that stated, "This probably will be the last message you will get from Peru." The message requested coffins, food and clothing and continued, "Two hundred or more are drowned and the remainder of the residents are waiting for daylight."[42] Although the 1913 flood caused devastation across the state, by most accounts, Peru suffered more than any other place in the state. An *Indianapolis Star* reporter who visited the city after the floodwaters had receded noted that the entire city had been submerged except for a small portion of the business district. A young man who assisted in the rescue efforts described the town as two small islands that folks tried to reach for safety. Boats paddled through the "Niagara" trying to rescue as many as possible. While some "suffered with a stoicism that had to be admired," others panicked, feeling there was no hope, and jumped overboard. Indeed, some of the rescue boats capsized as they tried to maneuver the rushing water, protruding treetops and passing debris. People who had found a safe place watched as the water swept through the city, destroying businesses and merchandise, carrying away homes and leaving anything that remained in ruins and covered in mud.[43]

The circus, which had its winter quarters in Peru, lost most of its animals. The sounds of lions, panthers, tigers, camels, horses and elephants trying to escape from their cages and stalls, along with the sounds of gunshots, added to the cacophony. The assistant superintendent of the Wallace Circus Farm reported that twelve elephants had been released but that nine of them had either drowned or died from injuries. The other three, he presumed, were still roaming free. The Miami County Lumber Company caught fire,

Downtown Peru on South Broadway, circa March 1913. *Miami County Historical Society.*

East Fifth Street in Peru, circa March 1913. *Author's collection.*

A bird's-eye view of the flooding in South Peru on March 25, 1913. *Author's collection.*

creating a horrifying show for those who were watching from the safety of the courthouse square. Following this night of terror, men set out in boats to inspect and conduct further rescues. They reported back, saying they had seen bodies floating in the water, including those of a married couple who had tied themselves together to avoid separation. They also reported that people were searching for their family members and that they had found survivors marooned on rooftops or clinging to chimneys and trees. They told stories of boatmen who had demanded a high price for their rescue efforts, one of whom had been shot and killed for his gross insensitivity. Some two thousand Peruvians had found refuge on the island surrounding the courthouse square, but their situation after the flood only worsened, as they faced quarantine when cases of smallpox, diphtheria, measles, mumps and scarlet fever were reported. The water level began to fall on Thursday, but heavy snow was also falling. The first rescuers with boats arrived from South Bend, and they found a "heartrending" scene—hundreds of desperate people stranded on the courthouse square, three miles from dry land and without heat, light or fresh water in filthy and unsanitary conditions. Around them, currents of muddy water ranging from ten to twenty-five feet deep ran through the city's streets.[44]

A systematic search ensued once the waters began to recede, and the initial estimate that hundreds had died declined. Missing people were located—some on the hills on the north side of the Wabash. Yet the flood

Damaged buildings and homes in South Peru, circa 1913. *Miami County Historical Society.*

had directly claimed the lives of up to twenty-five people, and it had indirectly killed even more due to exposure and disease. During rescue missions that Friday, it was reported that twelve bodies were found in one home in south Peru. Approximately five hundred dead animals were found scattered in the water throughout the city, and they presented a disposal issue as well as a health risk. An estimated one thousand homes had been damaged, and the city, its business owners and its residents had incurred between $2 million and $3 million in damages.[45] The 1913 flood had left its mark in Peru.

FORT WAYNE AND ITS THREE RIVERS

Fort Wayne lies fifty-four miles northeast of Peru at the confluence of three rivers—St. Joseph's, St. Mary's and Maumee. Platted in 1822, the founders located the town in this place that had long been important to Native Americans and had served as a pioneer trading post and a U.S. military fort. Although Fort Wayne was nicknamed Summit City, its altitude was lower than the geography to the north and south; the reference to a summit reflects its location at the divide between two watersheds—the St. Joseph's, St. Mary's and Maumee Rivers flowing in a northeasterly direction to Lake Erie, and the Eel, Little and Aboite Rivers flowing in a southwesterly direction to the Wabash River. Geologists have noted that only about four feet of earth prevented the two river systems from mingling their waters and that, during times of high water, a canoe could be paddled across the prairie from one river to the next. In all likelihood, Allen County's prairieland is a filled-up lake that previously discharged its waters in both directions. The natural water sources not only provided vital transportation routes but also fostered important components for the survival of pioneer settlement. Boosters noted the riches offered by this outpost: rich alluvial soil for fertile farmland, dense forests for timber and plentiful and varied wildlife for hunting. The remnants of this landscape history also meant that city developers would be challenged by marshes and swamps—not to mention that they would be building a city in the rivers' floodplains.[46]

Fort Wayne's geographical location placed it at an ideal point along the canal route to unite Lake Erie with the Mississippi River. The promise of riches that would accumulate once the canal passed through town drew people to the area. By 1835, the section of the Wabash and Erie Canal linking Fort Wayne with Huntington had been completed. Community members had invested their futures in completion of the canal, and when the canal boat *Indiana*, commanded by Captain Asa Fairfield, successfully navigated from Fort Wayne to Huntington, it was cause for celebration. Indeed, even before reaching its destination, its passengers were dancing, drinking whisky and "getting funny." Fort Wayne sat at a crucial point along the route between Toledo, Ohio, and Lafayette, Indiana, which was in operation by 1843. A disastrous flood in January 1847 caused severe damage to the canal system, but by then, Fort Wayne's status as a center for commerce had been established.[47]

The 1847 flood was just one of the many that were witnessed by settlers in Fort Wayne, and each flood was reported as being higher and more damaging than any before. The high-water mark from the 1828 flood, which was carved into the trunk of a tree near the fort, had been used as a measure when designing the banks and bridges for the canal. Unfortunately, the 1847 flood far surpassed that level. In a city surrounded by waterways, flooding was to be expected, and yet, whether because of faith in human supremacy over nature or because of faulty memories, city engineers, planners and developers forged ahead. By 1913, Fort Wayne's population had grown to over sixty-four thousand, and the spring flood was truly the worst flood in its history, as the high-water level reached 26.1 feet and remained above flood stage for ten days.[48]

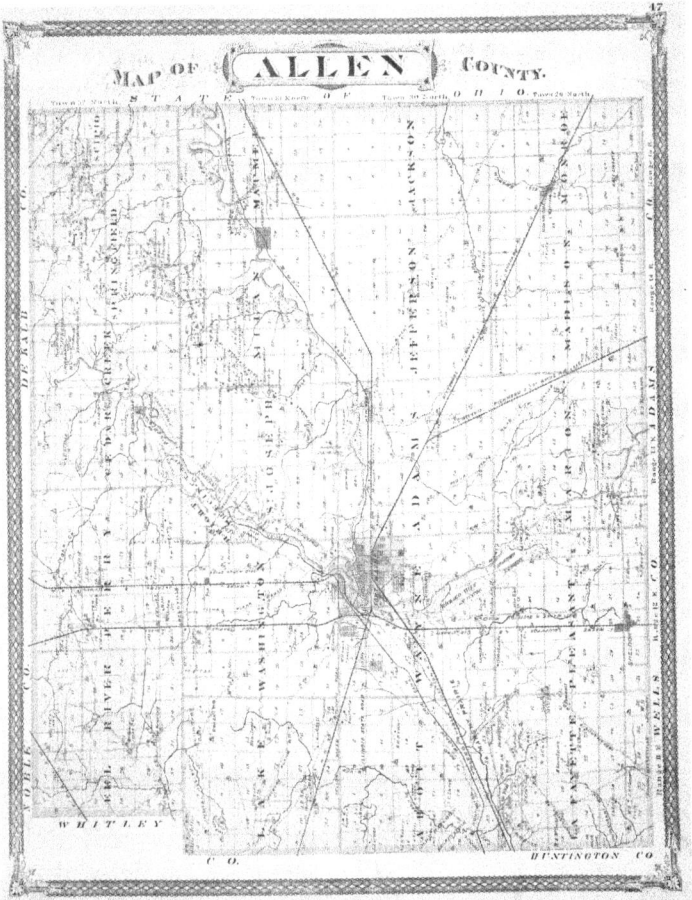

A map of Allen County, circa 1876, showing location of Fort Wayne and waterways. *Indiana Historical Society.*

The storm that began on Easter Sunday in 1913 delivered 4 inches of rain in two days, and by Monday afternoon, the rivers had poured into the city and already stood at more than five feet above flood stage. In total, 6.5 inches of rain fell on Fort Wayne over a five-day period with a devastating effect. Along with the rain, high winds, bitter cold and snow added to the misery that was experienced by people living in the flooded areas. Teams of boatmen worked to rescue those stranded in their homes, but a strong current made rescue missions dangerous. Six people lost their lives in the flood, including four young girls from the Allen County orphanage, who drowned when their rescue boat capsized. When the floodwater surrounded the orphanage and began to rise into the first floor, the township trustee called for rescue. The boatmen rowed up to the fire escape, where the children could descend into the boat. After six girls and their teacher were safely seated, the oarsman began to row away in the swirling water. As the orphans who were waiting their turn for rescue watched, a "swift flow struck the side of the boat," overturning it while still within one hundred feet of the fire escape. Despite the valiant efforts of the oarsman and the teacher, the raging water swept away four of the girls: Kitty Wise, six; Arda Woods, ten, along with her Bible (her "friend" she had brought with her); Alice Mannen, twelve; and Esther Kramer, twelve. A second boat reached the group and took the teacher and two surviving girls back to the home. With the teacher in serious condition, the doctor recommended that she be taken from the institution to her own home with the next boat, which was carrying four boys. The second boat had almost reached shore, but as it neared the Broadway Street bridge, another swift current capsized the boat. After a close call for one of the boys, all were saved, and further attempts to

A view of Main Street Bridge in Fort Wayne, circa March 25, 1913. *Allen County Public Library Community Album.*

remove the children from the home were discontinued. The next day, a U.S. lifesaving team from Evanston, Illinois, arrived to rescue the remaining fifty-five individuals who were stranded at the orphanage. As the boat was pulling away with its cargo, the last porch that was clinging to the home tore away in the rushing water—it was the same porch where the women and children had been waiting to be saved.[49]

A reported fifteen thousand residents of Fort Wayne were left homeless, and some 5,500 homes and buildings were either carried away, destroyed or suffered flood damage. The city's levees had failed, inundating the city's lowlands. The power plant flooded, leaving the city in the dark. The flood crippled all three of the city's water pumping stations, requiring residents to boil water carried from the river and placing the city in a precarious situation if a fire were to occur. The estimated cost of property damage amounted to $4.8 million (in 1913 currency), but the costs of the flood damage could not be measured by dollars alone.[50]

THE STORM IN THE CAPITAL

As previously described, Indianapolis had been established in a central location of the state in the floodplain of the West Fork of White River. In addition to the river, Fall Creek, Eagle Creek, Pogue's Run and Pleasant Run intersected the city. The landscape was flat with poor drainage and frequently flooded. By 1913, that fragile landscape was home to approximately 250,000 residents. A *Polk's City Directory* boasted that Indianapolis had become "the largest inland city in the country," and between 1890 and 1900, "the city had a percentage of growth larger than any other city in America of its class." Indianapolis was more than a "city of homes," however. As the directory described it:

> *It is a hustling, thriving business city, filled with up-to-date and progressive establishments and dotted thick with great and growing manufactories, which have experienced the greatest year's business in their history. That Indianapolis is attracting wide-spread attention in the world of manufacturing is evidenced by the fact that during 1905 no less than 89 different manufacturing plants were established in the city, many of them coming from other cities. At the present time the city has almost 2,300 manufacturing establishments, in which approximately 45,000 people are employed, receiving $15,000,000 in wages annually.*[51]

Industry brings environmental issues of one type, but the expanding number of people who accompany a booming industrial economy bring other types. Indianapolis hired Moses Brown, the outstanding sewerage engineer in the nation at the time, to plan a sewerage system for the city. By 1873, the city had constructed ten miles of conduits at an expense of $200,000. Similar to the systems that had been adopted in other cities during this time, the Indianapolis sewer system dumped into White River. The real purpose of the sewers was to drain stormwater to prevent flooding along the city streets. The city continued to rely on privies or mere dumping in the yard or alley for human waste disposal. By 1893, "the accumulated filth of one hundred thousand people was enough to turn the stomach," and the city hired Rudolph Hering, a New York sanitary engineer of national reputation, to devise a new system. Hering's plan provided for a citywide system of conduits with artificial and natural flushing, but the system still discharged its contents into White River.[52]

In addition, the city initially had no provision for the disposal of garbage or trash, which people simply buried in their yards or dumped into White River. By the end of the nineteenth century, the city's growth had created serious environmental problems for the river. Flooding took on more significance because floodwater was not only a nuisance, it was dangerously unhealthy. The river regurgitated what had been dumped into it by the city's residents and businesses. The 1907 Proceedings of the Indiana Engineering Society reported on the conditions of White River at and below Indianapolis:

> *A black deposit of oily, foul, animal and vegetable matter can be raised from the bed for miles. The weeds are coated with grease and with sewage plants. Flats are covered with blackening offal; driftwood collects dead hogs and other animal refuse where they putrefy. The odor is distinct for 40 miles down the river. Animals will not drink it. It cannot be used for the laundry or other domestic purposes when the cisterns and wells go dry.*[53]

In addition to the efforts made to gain control of refuse and human waste disposal, the city undertook another project shortly before the 1913 flood, which was influenced by the country's Progressive Era and City Beautiful Movement. George E. Kessler, a landscape architect and city planner who had been hired by the city in 1908, designed a park and boulevard system for Indianapolis. Kessler intended to manipulate the natural setting in Indianapolis to serve many functions at one time: improve quality of life and automobile thoroughfares, beautify the city and control flooding. He

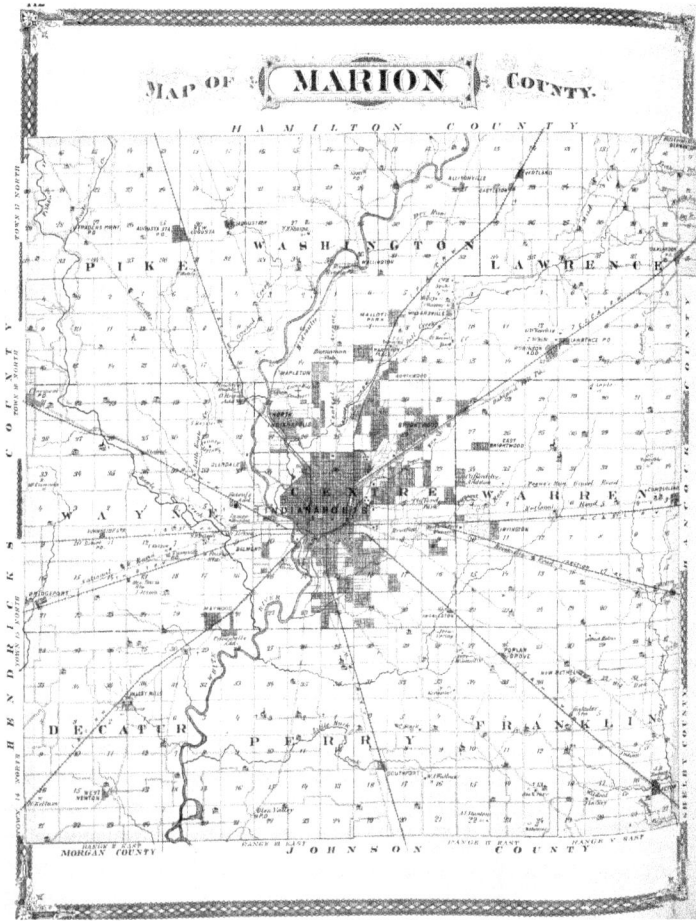

A map of Marion County, circa 1876, showing the location of Indianapolis and waterways. *Indiana Historical Society.*

wanted to "reclaim the garbage-strewn banks and polluted waters of streams in order to provide a natural beauty to the boulevards" based on methods he learned in Europe. Kessler applied his appreciation for the European form to the conditions in Indianapolis by merging the City Beautiful tenets of design with practical considerations, equally considering function and beauty.[54] This project and its goals were underway but had not been fully realized when the Great Flood occurred.

The rain began to fall in Indianapolis on March 23, and it continued for five days. The U.S. Weather Bureau's daily gauge readings on the West Fork of White River in Indianapolis showed the river level at a normal 4.7 inches on March 22, but it showed a rapid increase to 11.0 inches on March 24 and 18.0 inches on March 25. No further readings were available after the gauge was washed away sometime during the night of March 25.[55] Stories and photographs in the *Indianapolis News* showed flooded streets and submerged houses in multiple areas of the city, as flooding occurred not only along White River but also along Fall Creek, Eagle Creek, Pogue's Run and Pleasant Run. Fall Creek tore away the Meridian Street bridge, stone railing and part of the new boulevard. Unaware of the danger, the families who were living along Fall Creek's banks were awakened by militiamen and had to "desert their palatial homes."[56]

The flood did the most damage in the working-class neighborhood of West Indianapolis, a suburb that was annexed by the city in 1897 and was located southwest of downtown on the other side of the river. The low-lying area was inundated with overflows from both White River and Eagle Creek. In the early evening of March 25, water from White River crested

The North Meridian Street Bridge washed away by a flood in Indianapolis. *Jay Small Postcard Collection, Indiana Historical Society, P0391.*

and spilled over the banks, and West Indianapolis flooded east of Harding Street.[57] In some places, the water was between ten and fifteen feet deep. The flood washed away the tracks of the Belt Railroad from the Kentucky Avenue shops east to White River. The Union Stockyards were completely surrounded by water. A heavy current ran through the gap that was made by the break in the Belt Railroad levee.[58] Late in the afternoon on March 25, Mayor Samuel L. Shank notified Fire Company 19 at Morris and Harding Streets that the Morris Street levee was breaking. Within a few minutes, water began flowing into the fire station. By the time the firemen had hitched the horses to their wagons, the floodwater had reached their waists. The lower floor of the station, located a half mile from the river, was ultimately nine feet underwater.[59]

When the levee south of Oliver Street broke, the torrential waters drowned a man, woman and child in their own home. Two boatmen, one a police sergeant and the other a local resident, witnessed the drowning, but by the time they were able to row over to them, it was too late. These men and many others worked tirelessly to save stranded families from their roofs and attics. Some of their houses floated in the middle of the streets. Finally, at 1:30 a.m., the exhausted rescuers had to stop, although many people remained stranded. The news reported that "cries of distress were heard from all sides during the early hours of the night, but as the night wore on, the cries became fewer and feebler, and at 3:00 a.m., there was stillness in the flooded district."[60] Recalling the 1904 flood in Indianapolis, one reporter noted that this same area had been inundated, but it was just cornfields then. The levee built after that flood had been expected to provide the protection needed to build homes there.[61]

During the night of March 25, the rushing water swept away the Indianapolis & Vincennes Railroad bridge over White River. All efforts on the part of the railway employees to save the Vandalia bridge proved futile. The police, anticipating the bridge to be washed away, had backed five coal cars, two of them filled with bricks, onto the tracks to weigh the bridge down, but their efforts proved futile. On March 26, the raging river collapsed the east and middle spans of the West Washington Street bridge, which linked West Indianapolis to Indianapolis. The high-tension feed wires that supplied electricity for the Indianapolis Street Railway Company over the bridge were almost in the river at places. The bridge tore loose from the pier on the east end, and the roadway went below the water. The water ran over the road in torrents and gradually washed away parts of the railing.[62]

A break in the levee on White River in Indianapolis, circa March 27, 1913. *Indiana Historical Society, P0391.*

Interurban cars caught in the flood on West Michigan Street in Indianapolis, circa March 1913. *Bass Photo Co. Collection, Indiana Historical Society.*

The flood caused widespread havoc in the capital city. It stalled streetcars and interurban traffic, stranded passenger and freight train cars, interrupted telephone and telegraph services, made market news scarce, crippled businesses, closed schools, cut off the water supply, destroyed homes and rendered seven thousand homeless within a fifteen-mile area. In the ensuing terror-stricken hours and days, rescuers told of the grim horror of finding bodies in houses and seeing bodies floating in the water that could not be reached. The Associated Press reported estimates of the dead ranging from twenty to two hundred. By the end of the week, many of those who were originally missing or presumed drowned emerged from their places of refuge, but the flood and its aftereffects did claim lives in Indianapolis. The March 31 *Indianapolis News* listed the names of those who were confirmed dead. A volunteer boatman died from exposure after his boat capsized and he spent the night in the freezing water, clinging to a tree. Three individuals—a woman and two men—had drowned, and their bodies were found by search parties after the floodwaters receded. Three others—a man, woman and child—died due to exposure. A sixteen-year-old Shortridge High School student died of electrocution when he walked into a fallen telephone line while inspecting the flood damage with a friend.[63]

BEDFORD'S FLOODED STONE CITY

Bedford lies seventy-five miles southeast of Indianapolis in the rolling hills of Lawrence County, atop beds of limestone, flint, shale, coal and clay in a landscape that is intersected and penetrated by creeks, streams, the East Fork of White River, mineral springs, caves and sinkholes. In 1818, Lawrence County commissioners located the county seat on a bluff overlooking the river near the center of the county in a town named Palestine. Soon after settlement, the townspeople began suffering from malaria. Although they had constructed a courthouse, established businesses, built homes and entertained the hopes of becoming the state capital, they found that the graveyard was growing faster than the town. The town's alarming number of deaths prompted a search for a healthier location for the county seat. State legislators approved the relocation in 1825, and the appointed commissioners decided on the new location four miles northeast from the river. They named the new county seat Bedford and platted it to duplicate Palestine. The town was re-established in Bedford, and nature reclaimed the former site of Palestine. Bedford is nestled between the river to the south,

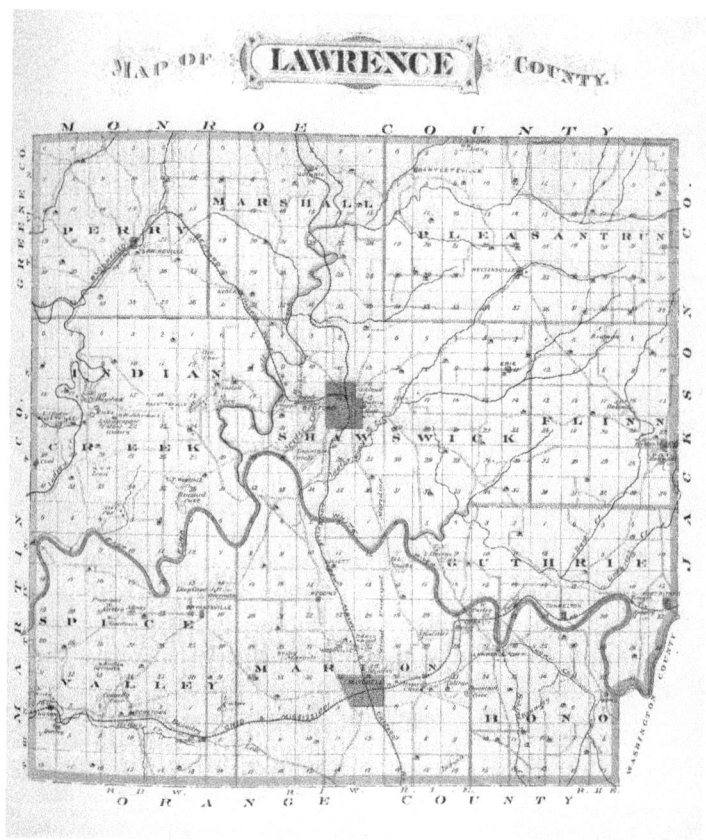

A map of Lawrence County, circa 1876. *Indiana Historical Society.*

Salt Creek and Spider Creek to the west and Leatherwood Creek to the east, and it sits atop some of the finest limestone in the world, which was formed from the fossils and shells remaining from an ancient lake.[64]

The riches beneath the town drove settlement in the area, and Dr. Winthrop Foote, one of the first settlers, promoted the future promises of a stone industry that would grow from this resource "so lavishly bestowed by the hand of the Creator." The stone was quarried for local buildings, and many of the extant structures in Bedford attest to this use. Shipping the stone to Chicago or New York, which had been Foote's vision, did not occur, however, until the railroads arrived. The first rail line through the county, the New Albany & Salem, was constructed between 1851 and 1853. After blasting out the stones, teams of oxen hauled them from the quarry for one mile to the railroad tracks. Other rail lines followed, including the critical twelve-mile-long Bedford Belt Railway, which was completed in 1893 and stretched across scenic, yet treacherous, terrain to connect quarries with the main rail lines. Advances in technology, communication and marketing techniques helped improve the success of these stone industry entrepreneurs. By the 1910s, Bedford had become the "Stone City," and the city and surrounding county boasted twenty-five of the largest cut-stone mills in the United States and sixteen quarries that were shipping to states across the country and to other countries, such as Canada, Cuba and the West Indies. Bedford's stone industry was an extensive operation and provided employment in quarries as cutters, millers and transporters. It also generated a boom in population.[65]

Unlike the flat land in the northern portion of the state, the hills of limestone in southern Indiana provided settlements with a natural drainage system. Regardless, in the process of converting the town into a modern city, people had also changed the environment. By 1913, Bedford's population had grown to around nine thousand. The hardwood forests that had covered the landscape when European settlers arrived had been cleared to construct the city and homes for residents. City administrators had graded and paved streets and sidewalks for fifty-two city blocks, installed underground cisterns for fire protection and built sewers and drains. Downtown Bedford displayed beautiful limestone buildings, including its courthouse, Carnegie library, post office, banks and churches. In addition to its stone industry, mills, distilleries, pork packing houses, hatteries, furniture factories and many other industrial operations comprised the city's commercial enterprises. Four rail lines ran through and around the city. The landscape had changed, and the natural drainage system had been interrupted.[66]

Mentions of flooding in the volumes of older history books are few, yet Bedford lies in the river floodplain—in the crosshairs of the Wabash and Ohio River drainage basins—and the porous limestone beneath the city could only absorb so much water at one time. The landscape reached that limit in 1913. Bedford's residents watched as a wind and rainstorm arrived in their city on Monday, March 24. After receiving four inches of rain overnight, the *Bedford Daily Mail* reported the next day that the city was isolated, with the river and streams already at flood stage, bringing back memories of the

"McKinley" flood sixteen years earlier, in 1897. Water surrounded the city and washed out roads and railways, and the accompanying wind knocked down trees and chimneys and tore off roofs. On Tuesday, White River had risen to twenty-four feet and was flooding businesses and homes. The *Daily Mail* described some incidents from around town: the Freidman shoe store had not only lost its roof and storefront windows, but it also had a foot of water in the store; the Pitman coal yard was under two or three feet of water; the family living on Seventeenth Street, between H and I Streets, had water up to their floorboards, and twenty-five of their chickens had drowned in the backyard coop; and the family in the house by the Salt Creek bridge had to vacate by boat.[67]

By Wednesday, Salt Creek had risen ten feet above the 1897 level, and White River was touching those high-water marks. Expectations were that the water would continue to rise, smashing records from the McKinley flood. Water surged into the pumping station, cutting off the water supply for days. All lines of communication with the outside world were lost. A local physician watched as the raging Salt Creek tore away the Williams Road bridge and carried it off around the creek bend.

A covered bridge over Salt Creek, between Bedford and Oolitic, circa March 1913. *Lawrence County Museum of History and Edward L. Hutton Research Library.*

Bedford Water Pump Station, circa March 1913. *Lawrence County Museum of History and Edward L. Hutton Research Library.*

Water overtook the Southern Indiana Power Company pump house at Williams Dam, which had been constructed in 1910 and 1911, cutting off electrical power to Bedford and the stone industry. Headwaters covered a landmark house that had been built in 1836 by the founders of the milling business in Bedford (although the heavy chimneys did their part to keep the house from floating away). A culvert under the Monon tracks caved in, creating a dammed-up lake. Water rose to the top of a farmer's barn loft, ruining 1,500 bushels of corn in the crib, but the farmer was able to move his animals to higher ground in time to save them. With White River rising eight inches an hour on Wednesday, property owners and city officials scrambled to save belongings and secure threatened infrastructure, including one of the county's oldest and most reliable bridges, the Rawlins Mills bridge, which was considered the best bridge of its kind, unlike the "modern flimsy steel bridges."[68]

The East Fork of White River did not crest until Saturday, March 29, at a record 47.50 feet. Bedford was luckier than other places in that no lives were lost. Still, Bedford suffered serious damage. Invoking a reference to the Biblical flood, the front-page headline of the *Daily Mail* that Thursday proclaimed, "And the Waters Prevailed and Increased Greatly Upon the Earth: All the High Mountains that Were Under the Whole Heaven Were Covered." When the creek began to fall, the Rawlins bridge settled back one inch out of line with minimal structural damage thanks to the quick-thinking actions of Mr. Sears, who anchored the bridge with cables before it could float away. However, many other structures that had withstood earlier floods were no match for the 1913 flood.[69]

LAWRENCEBURG FACES ITS "GREATEST FOE"

The 1913 storm reached places in the southeastern corner of the state as well. These places were not only downstream of the Wabash River and its many tributaries, but they were also within the Ohio River Basin, which forms the state's southern border. The site that was claimed for the city of Lawrenceburg in 1801—on the banks of the Ohio River, just below the mouth of the Great Miami River—seemed to be a prime location for a city and county seat. The site was flat and did have indentations where water would stand during spring months, but the founders believed they had platted the town above the Ohio River flood level. The location proved beneficial for the young city, and by 1820, Lawrenceburg's wharf and businesses were conducting a bustling river trade with New Orleans and the country in between. Unfortunately, flooding had been, as Dearborn County historian Archibald Shaw called it, the city's "greatest foe." If not for frequent overflows, which hampered the residents' abilities to conduct business and gave an advantage to competitors, some speculated that Lawrenceburg would have become a larger city.[70]

The city's first major flood, which broke all earlier records and delivered significant property damage, occurred in 1832. This flood, along with a national economic depression between 1837 and 1839, brought hard times to the area. Optimism about a new road to Indianapolis, the coming of railroads and the Whitewater Canal helped carry the city's people and businesses through those years. These new avenues meant that trade could expand north without solely relying on river transportation. The second major flood occurred in 1847, and it inundated Lawrenceburg. As they had in 1832, the people and businesses recovered, and the city continued to grow and prosper. Yet flooding continued to plague the city, and flood damage grew more severe. Three consecutive years of devastating floods—1882, 1883 and 1884—caused the city to face major setbacks. The 1884 flood surpassed all earlier floods, with the Ohio River reaching a height that was six feet above its previous high-water level from 1832, and reportedly, "many of the factories and businessmen never fully recovered from the losses" of the 1880s. Although the city's population had continually increased in prior decades, for the first time, the 1890 census reflected a decrease, as some decided to try their luck elsewhere.[71]

In early 1913, Lawrenceburg residents saw two flood events that changed the historical records. In January, heavy rains and melting snow caused the Ohio River to reach a height of sixty-two feet, which was not

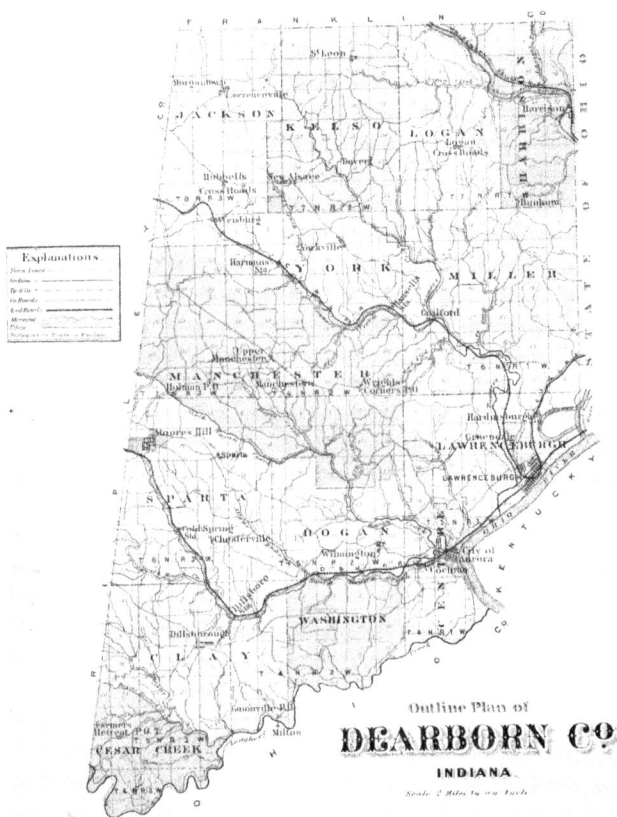

A map of Dearborn County, circa 1875. *Indiana Historical Society.*

an alarming height given that the townspeople had survived a height of sixty-six feet in 1907. Water had not entered the city since 1884, but in 1913, the rushing waters proved to be too much for the lower levee, despite its recent reinforcements following the 1907 flood. A night watchman, who was seated by a fire on top of the levee, noticed the ground start to give way and ran to the Newtown Engine House to ring the fire bell and warn the town. The January 22, 1913 edition of the *Lawrenceburg Press* reported that the watchman's brave actions saved the lives of many, as the embankment eventually slid away, leaving an opening that was sixty feet wide by eighty feet long and twenty feet deep. Local residents also understood the significance of the fire bell, and flood preparations were ingrained not only in their psyches but also in their actions to protect their homes, businesses and town. Plans were made to rebuild and reinforce the levee again, as it was called "Lawrenceburg's most important asset."[72]

Two short months later, another flood challenged the town's preparedness. Writing in 1915, Shaw noted that the March 1913 flood gained worldwide attention, with postcards calling it "the greatest disaster of modern times." Shaw stated that it was without precedent and that it "descended on an unsuspecting and unprepared people as the proverbial lightening from a clear sky." In Lawrenceburg, Easter Sunday had been a beautiful, balmy day, but rain arrived the following day. In a seventy-two-hour period, the area received eleven inches of rain, which the Great Miami, Whitewater and Ohio Rivers could not hold. By Wednesday morning, all the bridges on the Miami and Whitewater Rivers were gone, including the new "gigantic steel bridge" over the Miami River. The embankments that had been built for railroad tracks and bridge spans created barriers that only increased the fury of the rushing rivers, and

A view from the courthouse, looking west, in Lawrenceburg, circa 1913. *Collection of Jenny Awad, Dearborn County State Historian.*

Men on the second-story landing at Odd Fellows Hall and Opera House on High Street in Lawrenceburg, circa 1913. *Collection of Jenny Awad, Dearborn County State Historian.*

the rivers eventually overthrew everything in their way. Although the townspeople were hopeful that the reinforced levees would hold, families rushed to evacuate themselves and their belongings.[73]

In the early morning hours of Saturday, the factory whistles blew, warning that the levee was giving way. The water ripped an opening in the levee that was two hundred yards wide, through which the water "rushed with a force of a Niagara," carrying away houses and businesses with it. Families huddled in the courthouse, school buildings and engine house as the water flowed through town, covering High Street. Lawrenceburg residents joined the plight of so many others, as they were isolated without railroad, telephone or telegraph connections for two days. The town remained covered in water for seven days; then, finally, on the eighth day, the water began to recede from High Street, revealing the slimy mud that was left behind. When a government barge delivered relief provisions to Lawrenceburg on March 31, the crew found only "forty of the five thousand homes there not under water." Despite the extensive property damage, reports noted that only one person lost their life due to drowning, giving credit to the town's attention to preparations and warning systems.[74]

DEVASTATION ACROSS THE STATE

By the time the storm exited the state, it had impacted everyone in Indiana to some extent. Although the northernmost region of the state did not experience the heavy rainfall and damage that was seen in the rest of the state, places like South Bend, Hammond and Michigan City participated in relief efforts and sent reporters to bring back news and raise awareness of the suffering of fellow Hoosiers.

The entire Wabash Valley reported flood conditions. In the city of Wabash, the river broke the previous record from 1883; cut off gas, water, lights, communication and transportation; and left 750 people homeless. Property loss was estimated at $350,000. In Logansport, the combination of flooding from the Wabash and Eel Rivers claimed the life of one person, carried away ten houses, washed away bridges and cut off communication. In Lafayette, the floodwaters washed away two bridges over the Wabash River, along with the people who were standing on them. As the river continued to rise, it broke through a levee near Purdue University and overtopped another, isolating West Lafayette. Among the rescue workers were two young men who were attending Purdue University. As they were trying to reach two men marooned on a levee, their canoe overturned. One of the students managed to reach a telephone wire and swung to safety, but the other young man drowned in the Wabash River.[75]

Along White River and its tributaries, the cities of Noblesville, Elwood, Anderson, Muncie, New Castle, Rushville, Shelbyville, Bloomington and Washington were all affected by flooding. In Washington, a railway trestle over Prairie Creek collapsed while a work train was crossing. Four of the workers, including the engineer, drowned. Two of the rail workers were later rescued after floating two miles down the creek on cross ties, and another forty "narrowly escaped drowning."[76]

The rainstorm and flooding that followed high winds caused considerable damage to buildings and infrastructure in Richmond, which is intersected by the East, Middle and West Forks of Whitewater River. Local newspapers reported on the evacuation of the residents of the area of town known as Happy Hollow, where water had risen to the second stories of some homes. The tales of damage included the overflowed sewer system, flooded city power plants, the loss of a landmark covered bridge, the demolition of the old Nixon Paper Mill, the flooding of buildings and the loss of lumber at the Starr Piano Plant. Local bridges suffered crippling damage, including railroad bridges and the West Tenth Street bridge, effectively cutting off

Rescue work in Logansport by cadets from Culver Military Academy in nearby Marshall County, circa March 1913. *Indiana Historical Society, P0475.*

access to Reid Memorial Hospital. The *Richmond Palladium* headline declared that this flood was the greatest on record.[77]

Muncie, which is about fifty miles northeast of Indianapolis and encircled on three sides by the West Fork of White River, did not escape the 1913 flood. The rain began on Sunday and continued into Monday. Despite flooded streets and basements and interrupted train and interurban car service, on Monday, the levees were still protecting the city from the worst of it. On the same day, the *Muncie Evening Press* focused its attention on flooding reports that were arriving from neighboring counties—Marion, along the Mississinewa in Grant County; Portland, along the Salamonie in Jay County; and Union City, along the Little Mississinewa in Randolph County. In Johnstown, a suburb of Marion, a sixty-year-old "colored" man—a Civil War veteran who was well known—was reported "dead of fright" when he died while running up his stairs at 3:00 a.m. to escape the impending flood. On Tuesday, as the rain continued, Muncie suffered a flood that broke the previous record, which had occurred nine years earlier on the same day. The city had strengthened the levees after the 1904 flood, and flooding since then had not challenged the levees—that is, until 1913. The "yellow, angry torrent" overtopped the levees, submerged lowlands, crept into homes, entered businesses, shut off the city water

Flooded "Happy Hollow" neighborhood in Richmond, circa March 1913. *Wayne County Historical Museum.*

Main Street in Richmond, circa March 1913. *Wayne County Historical Museum.*

A bird's-eye view of the Pittsburgh, Cincinnati, Chicago and St. Louis Railroad Depot at Muncie, showing buckled tracks and stranded people, circa March 1913. *Indiana Historical Society, P0475.*

pumps, collapsed bridges, washed out streets and destroyed rail lines. At Beech Grove Cemetery, the river connected with a lagoon to form a big lake on the cemetery grounds. The swollen White River also claimed the life of a forty-year-old man who had been dislodging floating timber to save the High Street bridge. The water slowly began to recede on Tuesday evening but not before it had a devastating impact, and then, it left behind "a trail of filth and slime."[78]

Rushville, located along Flatrock River in Rush County, experienced the worst flood in its history in 1913. The water rose twenty-five inches higher than the highest flood measurement that the O'Neal brothers had been recording for years near their store on South Main Street. At 4:00 a.m. on Tuesday, the fire bell sounded to warn people of the rising river. Police and night watchmen tried to rouse business owners who had stores downtown. The water filled basements and cellars in the business district, damaging goods that had not been moved in time. Despite the previous warning markers, the O'Neal brothers' building flooded, and the owners reported major losses, including an estimated $6,000 of seed. The river continued to rise throughout the day, and at its highest point, it almost surrounded the courthouse. From the courthouse tower, the city appeared to be an isthmus with water as far as the eye could see to the south, east and west. The

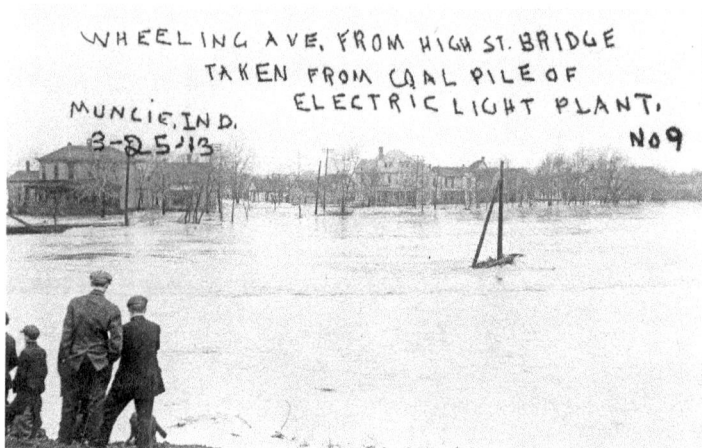

Wheeling Avenue from High Street bridge in Muncie, circa March 1913. *Ball State University Archives and Special Collections.*

flood washed out railroad lines, tore up streets and washed away bridges. Schools closed because the furnace could not be lit, and many children were stranded in their homes anyway. The factory district, which was underwater, closed shop. People who could not make it home before the water rose stayed with friends, and those at home moved upstairs or waited for rescue. The *Rushville Republican* partnered with the *Daily Jacksonian* to publish the news after the *Republican*'s equipment was damaged in floodwater. An early, conservative estimate of the damage put the costs at $250,000. The flood also claimed the life of one man in Rushville. James Hubbard, who was described as a "colored" man who was a horse trainer and employee of Lambert and McMillin, was driving a horse-drawn buggy to a repair shop on South Perkins Street; just after passing the jail, the water became too high to control the horse. Hubbard jumped into ten feet of water and attempted to swim back, but the undercurrent proved to be too much for him as the horrified crowd helplessly watched.[79]

In Brookville, at the confluence of the East and West Forks of Whitewater River, the night watchman sounded an alarm at 2:00 a.m. on Tuesday morning as water broke through the levee, flooding the valley. The floodwater claimed fifteen lives, although four persons' bodies were never recovered. Eight of the individuals whose lives were lost were members of the prominent Fries family; they ranged from six months to seventy-nine

The flooded business district in Rushville, circa March 1913. *Indiana Historical Society, P0408.*

years in age, crossing three generations. When the funeral for six of the Fries took place on Monday, March 31, it was "a sight never to be forgotten," as four caskets carried their bodies, with the six-month-old daughter held in one casket in the arms of the mother and the two young boys held in one casket. A *Brookville Democrat* reporter struggled to find the words to describe the devastation seen in Brookville following the levee breaks. Rescuers in boats battled the swirling water to reach people on rooftops and in second-story windows. The high water had swept away five bridges. An estimated 250 homes were flooded, and between 30 to 50 others had floated away. The local paper mill had water to the top of the first-story windows, and its brick warehouse had collapsed; the planing and saw mill had suffered considerable damage and had lumber float away; the furniture company's first floor had eight feet of water; and the electric company's machinery was damaged by the rising water and was not operational for a week to ten days, when new parts could be delivered from Cincinnati. Indiana's Lieutenant Governor W.P. O'Neill inspected the flood district in Brookville on April 5 and reported that, based on its size, "Brookville was harder hit by the flood than any place he had visited."[80]

In Martinsville, located on the West Fork of White River in Morgan County, the downpours began on Sunday, stopping work at the VanCamp factory. As the rain continued on Monday, workers were kept busy sweeping

The flood at Brookville in South Basin Hill (the old Whitewater Canal Basin), circa March 1913. *Indiana Historical Society, P0468.*

water out of the factory, while downtown, the lobby of the First National Bank became a waystation for bank clerks and other downtown workers. Mayor C.H. Hastings was kept busy laying down boards for temporary walkways. On Tuesday, the flooding became more serious in nature. As covered by the *Reporter-Times*, residents expected flooding, but the volume of water "astonished nearly everyone." The river was "on a rampage," and some claimed it had risen higher than it had during the August 1875 record flood. People living in lowlands, who had doubted the possibility of a flood of this magnitude and did not leave, were trapped in their homes. Word arrived from Indianapolis to the north that, based on the amount of rain received there, Martinsville should expect more water to come its way. The state ditch also overflowed its banks and became a swift and dangerous waterway. Sewers clogged with sand washing down from the hills, and cellars and furnace rooms filled with water. The city council called an emergency meeting on Tuesday to prepare for what was yet to come. Indeed, the river continued to rise throughout the day and night, shutting down the power plant, forcing more people from their homes, causing guests of the Martinsville Sanitarium to vacate, drowning livestock and washing out roads, railways and bridges. Martinsville had also flooded in 1881, 1882, 1898 and 1904, but the 1875 flood stood as the worst in memory. Once the river began to recede that Thursday, some residents debated whether the 1913 flood was higher and checked stakes that had been driven into bridges and other markers that had been left after the 1875 flood. In some places, the 1913 flood was lower; in others, it was higher.[81]

Columbus, situated at a point where the Driftwood and Flatrock Rivers converge to form the East Fork of White River in Bartholomew County, experienced serious flooding. The front page of the March 27 *Columbus Republican* declared that the flood of 1913 was worse than the flood of 1898, and at noon, the river was still rising. The weather station at Columbus reported receiving almost ten inches of rain, along with lightning strikes, in a five-day period. Trains, traction cars and mail were unable to enter or leave the city due to washouts on the Pennsylvania, Big Four, and Indianapolis, Columbus and Southern Traction Lines. Residents suffered immense losses and damages to their homes, barns, crops, horses and livestock. A levee on Haw Creek broke at 4:00 a.m. on Tuesday, releasing a rush of water that caught many off guard. The water trapped one man in a tree for several hours before he could be rescued by stringing a wire across to him; he had been out in the early morning hours, helping a friend move his cattle from the barn to higher ground. A torrent of water rushed through East Columbus, carrying everything with it, including small buildings. Factories reported

Men and a rowboat in front of H.E. Rutledge Grocery in Martinsville, circa March 1913. *Indiana Historical Society, P0326.*

damaged buildings and losses of inventory, equipment and merchandise. A new concrete bridge at Seventh Street could not withstand the raging Haw Creek, and its engine washed away, as did the power plant's smokestack and the woodwork around the bridge, leaving the iron structure out of line. County commissioners estimated that $50,000 would be needed to repair the bridges and roads in the county. Although the total cost of damages incurred by individuals, businesses and the government was inestimable, Columbus did not lose any lives to the flood.[82]

In Vincennes, which is situated on the Wabash River on the western border of the state, residents experienced the same high winds and heavy rain that the residents of Terre Haute had experienced. The river had risen rapidly, and by Tuesday, it had inundated North Vincennes. Predictions were that the record height of 23.0 feet would soon be surpassed. Already, the town had lost telephone and train service, and town trustees were busy directing rescues by wagons and boats. By Saturday, the river had reached a crest of 24.2 feet, broke through three levees and flooded seven hundred homes. The cost of the damage was estimated at $500,000. On Sunday, March 30, Governor Ralston received an urgent request from Vincennes for two hundred tents to provide some protection for the homeless. The train delivering the tents was not able to reach Vincennes until Monday, leaving the refugees to spend Sunday night outdoors in cold and wet conditions.[83]

After the rain stopped, the rivers and streams continued to rise, with accumulating water causing more damage. Rainwater collected in the Wabash and Ohio Rivers in the southwest corner of the state. It was not until the following week that the rivers reached their full potentials in places like Hazelton, East Mount Carmel, Mount Vernon, New Harmony and Evansville. An embankment on the Wabash River broke during the night of Saturday, March 29, inundating New Harmony, whose main street remained covered with five to six feet of water until the following Tuesday. Rescuers in skiffs had been working to get refugees, who they found stranded in second stories and on roofs, to safety. Hazelton's residents also found themselves in dire circumstances, with those living in isolated farmhouses difficult to reach in the backwaters of White River. Refugees crowded into churches and schoolhouses in Hazelton. The news they heard was that White River had formed a new channel and cut away a quarter mile of railroad tracks, which would leave the town cut off from river access. On March 31, Mount Vernon's mayor sent a wire to Governor Ralston requesting assistance from Indiana's National Guard to set up a refugee camp. The mayor reported, "Hundreds of flood sufferers from the

Wabash River bottoms are flocking to Mount Vernon, and the worst of the flood is yet to come."[84]

A news report from Evansville on Tuesday, April 1, called the southwest corner of the state a "sea of water." Situated on an oxbow in the Ohio River, buildings along the city's riverfront were threatened on Wednesday, April 2, when high winds combined with high water. The river had reached a level close to the city's worst flood in history, which had occurred in 1884, and the river was still on the rise. Predictions were dire, with more rain forecasted for that evening. At 6:00 a.m. on Friday, April 4, the night watchmen fired shots and rang the church bell to warn residents in the Howell and Inglewood neighborhoods that the new levee had been cut. After workmen had spent four days constructing the levee, they decided to make a cut in the levee to avoid a more dangerous break and the certain loss of lives. An estimated two thousand homes had been flooded, many people had fled to higher ground, water flowed through an estimated twenty miles of city streets, streetcars were not operational, several factories had closed because of the high water and the high school gymnasium and technical training school were underwater. The Ohio River did not crest at Evansville until Saturday, April 5, when it reached 48.40 feet—just five inches below the 1884 record. At that time, the *Evansville Press* announced that the danger was over. In typical style, the *Press* reported on circulating rumors of further devastation and near-hysterical women's reactions, but it reassured its readers, "By Sunday, the river will begin to crawl back into its kennel." The river was slow to recede, however, and had only fallen by one foot on Tuesday, April 8.[85]

In Medora, a news photographer captured the sad scene of cattle lying in a field after drowning when the East Fork of White River left its banks. The farmer had lost about $10,000 worth of cattle. A farmer in Landersdale reported that he had lost 150 head of hogs. A farmer near Mount Vernon said he had lost 260 acres of wheat on the Indiana side of the Wabash River and another 120 acres on the Illinois side. Large landowning farmers were in a better position to bear these losses, but tenant farmers, who lost their shares of the previous year's crops and provisions, were left in a more vulnerable position. A committee was formed to seek federal assistance for the "penniless, starving tenants" in the lowlands of the Ohio and Wabash River Valleys, resulting in the American Red Cross apportioning $15,000 to the Mount Vernon area, $4,500 to New Harmony and $4,000 to Griffin to help reimburse farmers for their property losses. Many farmers across the state suffered damage not only when they lost livestock, crops, buildings and equipment, but also when floodwaters washed away topsoil and left behind gravel and debris.[86]

It is impossible to tell every story from across the state or even the many stories from one location. Hundreds—if not thousands—of reports overwhelmed news gatherers. Widespread fear and speculation played a significant role in the information and types of stories printed in the first few days of the storms. The damage to lines of communication did not help matters. People anxiously awaited news about not only local situations but also friends, family and neighbors in other towns. Often, when news did arrive, it was not good and added to their stress. A dispatch from Indianapolis announced that the Salt Creek had drowned several families in Brown County and caused $150,000 in property loss.[87] One rumor suggested that sixteen people had drowned at Evansville, while another claimed that seventeen houses had been washed away in Shoals.[88] Newspapers had reported all week that forty people had drowned at Brookville; although, by Saturday, the number of deaths had been adjusted to fifteen.

By the end of the first week, news began to arrive from places that had previously been silent. Salem had been completely isolated since Monday, except for a phone line to Louisville, Kentucky. The town had not lost any lives, but it had significant property damage. People learned that the small town of Vallonia had been underwater from the Muscatatuck and White Rivers.[89] Flooding and devastation in Dayton and cities across Ohio followed quickly on the heels of Indiana's experiences, and stories about Ohio began to dominate headlines in Indiana newspapers.[90] The initial reports were terrifying, and the focus on another state's suffering, especially a neighboring state from which the reports of devastation exceeded Indiana's, may have helped Hoosiers put their own suffering into perspective and know they were not alone.

TALES FROM SURVIVORS AND RESCUE TEAMS

Survivors shared their harrowing stories, providing more details of the flood's impact. In Moscow, a gray-haired couple in their seventies, who had been marooned in their home, surrounded by the swollen Flatrock River, were finally rescued after twenty-four hours and several failed attempts to save them. Seven men, their would-be rescuers, were, themselves, rescued the next morning, along with the couple, after the treacherous water had capsized their boats and they spent the night clinging to trees. Two of the men were found in critical condition from exposure, and they collapsed, unconscious, into the rescue boat. As the elderly couple was treated for cold exposure, they explained how they had escaped the water that was rising in their home by climbing into the stove, punching a hole through the ceiling and climbing into the attic to wait for help to arrive.[91]

In the case of two young people who had set out in a skiff to escape the rising water in Brookville by crossing the West Fork of White River, only the young woman arrived safely. The eighteen-year-old man had fallen overboard when the boat was upset close to shore, and he could not swim. He was able to hang on to the side of the boat for a while, but he eventually slipped into the icy water. His body was not recovered until three days later.[92]

A train crew traveling from Oolitic to Bedford found themselves stranded on the tracks on Tuesday. The next day, a few braved the high waves in a motorboat, but they "had a very exciting time in the midst of a tree top," convincing the others to wait another day until the water calmed.[93] Near Medora, after escaping her flooded home, a woman delivered her baby while floating in a boat without an oar and with only her husband in attendance. The couple's boat reached the bluffs safely with the mother and child in fine condition.[94]

North of Hope, two men who had attempted to rescue the millworkers who were trapped at the Charles Flour Mill along the raging Flatrock River on Tuesday found themselves in a compromised position. After their boat was capsized, they managed to grab onto some trees. What made their plight more newsworthy was their decision to remove their clothes before making the boat trip. They had reasoned that, if they fell into the water, they would be better equipped to swim without the additional weight of clothing. Another boat rescued one of the men from his tree later that evening, but they were not able to reach the second man. Onlookers saw him repeatedly slapping his naked body to revive himself. When he was finally rescued around noon on Wednesday, he was suffering from exposure and was barely able to hang onto the tree.[95]

The flood provided some people with memorable experiences that would last a lifetime. Peru reported that six babies were born to women among the 1,300 flood refugees staying at the courthouse. The women and babies were all doing fine.[96] One family, who lived in a small cottage near the railroad bridge spanning the river between North and South Peru, reported a terrifying night in their home; during the height of the flood, an elephant that had escaped the circus winter quarters frantically hurled itself against their cottage.[97] A rural mail carrier in Morgan County was making deliveries on Monday, March 24, when, as he was driving his wagon beside Stott Creek in search of a place to cross, the wagon suddenly turned over in deep water. He managed to cut the harness to release the horse, gather the mail and get to shore before the swift current caught his wagon and carried it down the creek. He had to borrow a wagon from a nearby farm and did not get back to Martinsville until 7:00 p.m. that evening.[98] A rescue worker in Indianapolis, who had experience in managing canoes in Alaska, survived a canoe rescue trip in West Indianapolis, but he reported that the "swirling mass of murky water" running through town was "more powerful than the rapids of the Yukon."[99] Then there was also a Presbyterian minister in Milroy who left on a mission to rescue an elderly couple from their houseboat without his coat. He was caught in a tree and spent the night there until he was found in the morning, unconscious and "half-dead" from exposure. Luckily, he had had the forethought to remove his suspenders and lash himself to the tree, which likely saved him.[100]

Rescue workers who had traveled to other towns to assist the residents there returned home with their own stories. Sixty-five agricultural students from Winona College and forty rowboats, under the supervision of Captain W.L. Reynolds, answered the telephone call for assistance from Peru. One of the young men returned home to Mishawaka and shared his experiences with a *South Bend Tribune* reporter. He explained that, after traveling as far as possible on an interurban freight car, the group had to row three miles to reach the flooded sections of Peru. They worked until midnight, rowing to flooded houses in the north and east sections of the city to rescue people and then take them to either the courthouse, the Carnegie library, city hall or one of the schools that was still above water. He told of the bravery—along with some amusing incidents—he had witnessed. By the time they reached one woman, the water had already risen to her shoulders, but she calmly climbed into the boat when asked. Another woman they encountered was knitting in her rocking chair with her feet in two inches of water, and she refused to leave her home of fifty-one years. The rescuers decided to return later to check on her. In another case, a man stuck his head out of his window and offered the group twenty-five dollars to first row two blocks away to feed his horse. They declined his offer and checked on him later. Along with these tales of human responses to the flood, the young man reported, "You have no conception of the conditions and the suffering of the victims.…[With] heat, light, food and drinkable water cut off, the conditions are appalling."[101]

TALLYING THE LOSSES

Often, the headlines about the flood were later determined to be misinformed or exaggerated. The initial confusion and terror of those who were at the epicenter of the storms played a role in the news that was shared with the outside world. Reports from national news services often included speculation and rumor about the conditions and number of deaths in Indiana, with stories circulating that corpses were floating down the streets of Peru and that 60 to 250 people had drowned there. Initial reports stated that between 200 and 1,500 people had drowned in Indianapolis.[102] Although the number of deaths was not as high as initially feared, the losses were significant.

The exact number of lives lost in Indiana, either directly or indirectly to the flood, has never been determined, but the official estimate stands at 200 people. Many people who were initially reported as missing were later found, and all of those stories could not be accounted for in the newspapers. One such incident in Indianapolis was followed by the *News*; a man was believed to have drowned Wednesday night while trying to swim himself and two horses from his flooded home on Nordyke Avenue. Witnesses saw the man and his horses get swept away by the water. On Friday, it was reported that he had been found by a rescue party in serious condition but alive. The bodies of the horses he had tried to save, however, were later discovered on Morris Street.[103] Records are scarce about the number of people who lost their lives in the following weeks after contracting illnesses from exposure to the wet and cold conditions or from contracting infectious diseases due to the unsanitary and wretched conditions following the flood. An estimated 200,000 people were rendered homeless across the state.

According to a report prepared from the U.S. Department of Agriculture, Weather Bureau, the total monetary losses in Indiana amounted to over $20 million (in 1913 currency), which included losses and costs to repair or replace the railroads and trolleys, highways and bridges, crops, livestock, industries and equipment and homes. Previously, the worst flood in the state had occurred in 1904, and the Weather Bureau used statistics from that flood for comparison. The rain in 1904 had lasted for two days, but in 1913, the rain continued for a five-day period. In addition, the average rainfall reported from seven stations across the White River Watershed was 4.19 inches in 1904 and 7.81 inches in 1913. Some locations received more rain within a single twenty-four-hour period in 1913 than they had in the total two-day period in 1904. Chart 4 shows the data from weather stations that reported over 5.00 inches of rain in a single twenty-four-hour period.[104] The 1913 flood had earned the title of the Great Flood.

CHART 4

WEATHER STATIONS REPORTING PRECIPITATION
IN EXCESS OF FIVE INCHES FOR TWENTY-FOUR CONSECUTIVE HOURS

Station	Amount	Date
Bloomington	6.56	March 25
Columbus	7.00	March 25
Elliston	6.10	March 25
Mauzy	5.59	March 25
Nashville	6.01	March 25
Seymour	5.43	March 25
Shoals	6.66	March 24
Washington	6.10	March 25

Courtesy of C.E. Norquest, "Flood in the White River of Indiana, March, 1913," in The Floods of 1913 in the Rivers of the Ohio and Lower Mississippi Valleys *(Washington, D.C.: Government Printing Office, 1913), 72.*

3.

IN THE WAKE OF THE FLOOD

The flood has served the purpose of welding the citizens into closer bonds of neighborliness…again emphasizing the fact that this is "No Mean City."
—*W.M. Herschell (1913)*[105]

Rescue and assistance for those directly impacted by the flood began immediately. Neighbors helped neighbors, and strangers helped strangers. The flooding called for an immense effort to overcome the human suffering it had left behind. Stories of heroism and beneficence on the part of fellow humans abounded. Other stories shed a less favorable light on folks, as survival instincts can take different forms. This chapter shares stories from both ends of the spectrum and everything in between. They are stories about people from next door, from different towns and from other states; from men, women and children; from different races and economic classes; and from individuals, organizations, businesses and governments. Together, they weave a story of what happened in the wake of the Great Flood.

RESCUE AND RELIEF

The extraordinary flood triggered an extraordinary response to help. The first line of relief came from those who braved the swift currents in boats and canoes to rescue stranded people. Anyone with a boat who was willing and able volunteered to help. People with summer lake homes fetched

A rescue crew from Michigan City in Peru, circa March 30, 1913. *Miami County Historical Society.*

boats to aid in the efforts. Police departments deployed their boats and commandeered boats from local boat companies. Trains delivered boats as close as possible to flooded areas. Groups from other towns volunteered to bring their boats to help in places that were considered to be in worse shape than their own towns. Some rescue attempts ended in tragedy, but there were far more successful rescues.

During those first stressful days, women provided an invaluable service answering emergency telephone calls and passing along messages. The March 26 edition of the *Martinsville Reporter-Times* commended the young women who were employed by the telephone company, as they had worked day and night and "experienced all manner of inconveniences" but endured "a test that would discourage most men." The March 27 edition of the *Tipton Daily Tribune* praised the work of the "telephone girls," who had labored heroically day and night to help during the crisis. The paper noted that, although some complaints and "unkind remarks" had been made about the service, the girls did not deserve any criticism, as the lines were in such bad shape it was a wonder they were able to get any connections. The Mount Vernon Relief Association president also called attention to the "telephone girls," who answered thousands of calls and passed along messages to "relief men" to prevent "loss of life, hunger and despair."[106]

One important task was finding missing people and reconnecting them with family and friends. In the chaos of the flood, people found shelter wherever possible, often fleeing to higher ground. Until the missing could be accounted for with accurate and reliable information, rumors of the number of deaths could not be dismissed, but the lost lines of communication did not help matters. Relief committees set up a central location to coordinate this work. In Indianapolis, the general relief committee established an information bureau in Tomlinson Hall. The committee posted a notice on the front page of the March 28 edition of the *Indianapolis News* asking every refugee to stop by or call and register their name so that information could be given to family and friends who inquired as to their whereabouts.

Attending to the needs of those who were left homeless was another pressing matter. In Indianapolis, the mayor ordered the conversion of Tomlinson Hall into a temporary shelter and hospital. Homeless people from Indianapolis and its surrounding suburbs were brought to the hall for care. Fort Benjamin Harrison provided five hundred cots, mattresses and blankets. Citizen committees organized to raise money and to distribute food and clothing. Volunteer doctors and nurses attended to injuries and other medical needs, including an outbreak of contagious diseases. Pneumonia, whooping cough and measles were discovered among the refugees, and those who were infected were quarantined to prevent the spread of these diseases.[107]

City council members convened for emergency meetings to authorize relief funds and plans for relief efforts. Committees were set up to coordinate the work needed to address specific concerns and to distribute funds. On March 26, Indianapolis Mayor Shank created a committee of community volunteers—the Indianapolis General Relief Committee—to provide charitable relief and basic necessities to the affected families. This committee, along with other charitable organizations, collected contributions and worked to distribute aid to the flood victims. Subcommittees were created for relief in the form of food, fuel, clothing, housing, furniture, finances and publicity.[108]

Similar relief efforts occurred in cities across the state. The March 29 edition of the *Fort Wayne Gazette* ran an article praising the "little army of women" who had proven to be heroines to those in need. While the men kept track of the books and arranged for deliveries of provisions to various parts of the city, the women "worked untiringly, many without even stopping for a bite to eat or a moment's rest" to sort and arrange food and clothing and fill the requests of the flood victims who were pouring in day and night.

The bread line at the courthouse in Peru, circa March 1913. *Author's collection.*

The reporter described the great need represented by the victims, calling many cases pathetic; yet they were not poor, just temporarily without food, clothing and shelter.

Local religious groups played an invaluable role in the relief efforts. They threw open their doors to the homeless, served meals and offered spiritual support. Father Joseph Weber opened the Assumption Church in West Indianapolis as a temporary home for over three hundred people who found themselves homeless after the flood. He also helped deliver a message of the suffering in this working-class neighborhood to the rest of the city: "Only those of us who live among and know the poor can appreciate the great suffering and the great need of assistance….They are all good at heart, and it is the fault of society, mainly, that they are placed in such a position that they cannot help themselves when calamity falls upon them." Reverend Weber served as a mediator and coordinator in the rescue and salvage efforts, and he offered the rectory at Assumption Church to serve as a Red Cross station.[109]

The goodness of friends and neighbors cannot be underestimated. The March 28 edition of the *Evansville Press* noted that the "colored citizens of Evansville voluntarily jumped into the relief work for Indiana's flood stricken," and a committee was collecting funds that would be turned over to the treasurer. During an interview later in her life, Adeline Claighorn Haine, who, at the age of thirteen, experienced the flood in West Indianapolis, remembered that her family originally went to the Salvation Army until her school teacher spotted them and insisted that Adeline, her mother and her two sisters stay with them.[110]

Organizations wanted to help the people who were suffering in their own communities and in others. The Masonic bodies in Indianapolis prepared five hundred "ration" bundles for distribution in West Indianapolis; they were to be handed out to the flood sufferers whether they were members of the order or not. Each bundle contained bacon, coffee, beans, rice, sugar, a can of milk, two loaves of bread, two blankets, "comforts" and socks and stockings. The grand master of Indiana's grand lodge then sent telegrams to twelve cities that had been greatly affected, including Brookville, Peru, Kokomo and Jeffersonville, asking if they, too, needed relief.[111]

Communities that had suffered themselves offered help to others. The March 27 edition of the *Muncie Evening Press* reported on the work of Muncie's relief committee, which had organized donations from the city's residents for the flood victims in Peru. The donations of bedding, clothing, groceries, shoes, lanterns, oil and coal were loaded onto a train car and were accompanied by committee members and several physicians. The train backed into Peru as far as possible and waited for the provisions to be unloaded, hauled over the swollen Wabash River and then loaded onto waiting wagons, cars and trucks. The returning train brought news of the terrible conditions in Peru, and the committee began organizing a second relief train to leave the next day.

The Indianapolis General Relief Committee Chairman sent a telegram to Columbus Mayor Charles S. Barnaby on March 28, extending an offer of financial assistance. Apparently, Indianapolis residents had been generous enough in their contributions to the local need that the committee and residents could also "do something for others." Mayor Barnaby thanked the chairman for the kind offer but declined to accept, saying that the damage in Columbus had been slight "compared to other places."[112]

People from Indiana cities and towns that were not directly impacted by the flood were eager to help in any way they could. When asked by the Fort Wayne Commercial Club, the owner of the Rome City Rowboat Company immediately sent two train carloads of rowboats, with two pairs of oars each, to aid in Fort Wayne's rescue efforts. The following day, he sent another twenty rowboats when asked. The people of South Bend arranged to have train cars of meat, eggs and butter delivered to Fort Wayne and other cities in need. Mishawaka Mayor John A. Herzog issued a proclamation for that city's residents and civic, fraternal and church societies to assist Peru.[113]

Local businesses found ways to contribute to the relief efforts. The Empress Theater in Fort Wayne still had electricity, and it advertised in the March 27 edition of the *Fort Wayne Sentinel* that it would donate the entire proceeds—at ten cents per ticket—from one of its Friday afternoon matinees to the relief fund for flood sufferers. As noted in the advertisement, attending a show would "help swell the fund." The People's Outfitting Company issued a notice to its patrons in the March 28 edition of the *Indianapolis News* that the company would repair and refinish, without charge, furniture damaged by the flood.

Addressing the needs of flood survivors did not end when the floodwaters receded. After addressing the initial emergency needs of the flood survivors, the Indianapolis General Relief Committee turned its attention to what it referred to as the "larger task." The larger task involved the day-to-day future operations of households—the "tables, beds, chairs, pianos, kitchen cabinets and sewing machines" that were reported to be hopelessly damaged and generally in pieces throughout the flooded district. Much of the committee's work was assigned to the Women's Auxiliary Committee, which was working from its headquarters in downtown Indianapolis. The women's Personal Service Subcommittee took on the task of carrying "hope and cheer," visiting the sick in hospitals and generally assisting the flood victims with "friendly feeling and sympathy." When food distribution moved to the women's headquarters in early April, the committee reported that "more than eleven hundred persons were reached with food." The Sewing Committee made over sixteen hundred new garments, including dresses and diapers. The Colored Women's Committee provided food for over three hundred families, delivered clothing to over one hundred families, made more than one hundred new garments and collected donations for the general committee. The women's subcommittees for clothing, repairs and cleaning, transportation and communications also conducted crucial work to help restore living conditions in flooded districts. The Indianapolis committee continued this work until it was disbanded in December 1913.[114]

On April 15, Governor Ralston met with the American Red Cross director and representatives from relief committees from across the state. During the meeting, each relief committee shared the status of the relief funds it had collected and the work it had done, along with its current situation. The discussions only focused on the relief that was needed for individuals that could be addressed by the Red Cross—business losses were to be left for another meeting. The meeting highlighted the continued suffering in Indiana. In Lawrenceburg, 608 people remained homeless, and the committee was providing them with shelter in boxcars, public buildings and similar places. The committee also reported that 75 dwellings had been carried away, 51 had been destroyed and 128 had been taken off their foundations. The committee from Shoals reported, "Our people are poor." It also reported that 47 dwellings had been destroyed, with 30 of those having been washed away. From West Terre Haute, the city attorney reported that 350 families were destitute, and the average amount of aid provided to each family by the relief fund was $10.97. Brookville's committee reported 196 families driven from their homes, 38 houses had been categorized as "total wrecks" and that "85 percent of the people in the flood's path were laboring people." The committee estimated it would "take between $40,000 and $50,000 to put these people on their feet and replace the houses they [had] lost." In Logansport, 750 houses had been ruined. The committee had placed the loss for each family around $130, but the goal was to obtain contributions of $66.66 for each family to help bridge their situation.[115]

The generosity of fellow citizens, business owners, charitable organizations and government agencies had been great. Newspapers printed the names of donors and the amounts they contributed to the local relief funds, whether they contributed $0.25 or $500. Many of those who gave were sufferers themselves. This spirit of giving was certainly appreciated. Unfortunately, the need exceeded the amount received, and the lives lost could not be reimbursed.

FEDERAL ASSISTANCE

The Great Flood was sometimes also referred to as the Great Wilson Flood.[116] The flood occurred just a few weeks after President Woodrow Wilson's inauguration and presented a daunting challenge in the early days of his administration. Indeed, the enormity of the Great Flood called for federal assistance. On Wednesday, March 26, President Wilson sent a telegram to Governor Ralston, stating, "I deeply sympathize with the people of your state in the terrible disaster that has come upon you. Can the federal government assist in any way?"[117] Governors and mayors from across the impacted region—from Nebraska to Indiana and New York—accepted the president's offer and sent requests for specific needs. In the immediate wake of the flood, that assistance arrived as quickly as possible given the hampered railroads and swollen rivers.

Federal rescue and aid came in many forms, including troops, professional rescue teams, medical experts, federal agency liaisons, equipment, supplies, bureaucracy interventions and local order reinforcement. On March 26, newspapers reported the welcome news that President Wilson had ordered U.S. troops to be ready to deploy to the flood districts in Indiana and Ohio. Federal agencies began organizing relief expeditions to provide the affected states with food rations, tents, blankets, cots and medical supplies. Army posts in Philadelphia, Pittsburgh, St. Louis, Chicago and Fort Thomas (Kentucky) began loading these supplies for delivery to the devastated areas within twenty-four hours. U.S. Lighthouse Service employees near Louisville were ordered to utilize all of their available boats to aid in rescue and relief work. When residents of Canada wanted to send food, clothing and supplies to flood sufferers in Indiana and Ohio, Secretary of the Treasury William A. McAdoo waived the customs duty on those imports.[118]

From Washington, D.C., the president called the flood a "national calamity" and made a national appeal to anyone who was able to assist the American Red Cross—either in labor or by monetary contribution—noting, "We should make it a common cause. The needs of those upon whom this sudden and overwhelming disaster has come should quicken everyone capable of sympathy and compassion to give immediate aid to those who are laboring to rescue and relieve."[119] When the American Red Cross reached out to Governor Ralston, offering monetary assistance, he replied that the monetary contributions to the devastated districts would be most useful. Red Cross officials arrived in Indiana the following week to investigate the conditions after the flood and report back to Washington, D.C. With the officials' report of the damage, the national office would determine the amount needed for relief in Indiana based on a pro rata division of the funds collected by the Red Cross for flood sufferers.[120]

The federal government offered medical assistance to the state's public health workers, and the state accepted. On Thursday, State Board of Health Commissioner Dr. W.F. King sent a telegraph to the U.S. surgeon general, accepting assistance in "handling the impending disease wave" that he "expected to follow in the wake of the floods." Dr. King called the need urgent and added, "Indiana can use all help you can give."[121] Federal aid also helped with warding off disease in the wake of the flood. When federal health officer Dr. J.O. Cobb arrived in Indianapolis, he supported the city board of health's declaration to quarantine West Indianapolis in an effort to prevent the spread of disease. City police and militiamen did not have the power to enforce the demand, especially after Mayor Shank and Police Superintendent Martin J. Hyland defied the health officials' recommendation by removing the ropes that sectioned off West Indianapolis and allowing people to enter. Of course, people who lived in the district were anxious to check on their homes, to collect any salvageable items, to begin cleaning up and to protect their homes from vandals. However, sightseers also flowed into the district. With federal agreement on the wisdom of the health officials' approach, it gained additional weight and legitimization. To reduce the number of people leaving and entering the flooded district, Dr. Cobb recommended only allowing men to stay and conduct cleaning, while urging, "Women and children who were unable to withstand the rigors of life in a pestilence-threatened area be removed at once." Dr. J.N. Hurty, with the State Board of Health, also approved a quarantine order and noted that the state would be compelled to take action if the city could not.[122]

After assessing the situation in Indianapolis, Dr. Cobb planned to travel to other stricken cities, including Brookville and Lawrenceburg. The March 31 edition of the *Indianapolis News* reported that the doctor expected to make his way there partly by wagon and partly on foot. He would confer with health officers in each city and share his expertise in public disaster response. At the very least, he would deliver his principal message: boil water for drinking and cooking for several weeks after the flood. Another federal public health officer, Dr. Hugh De Valin, headed north to Peru, which had sent an urgent request for a sanitation expert. After arriving in Peru, Dr. De Valin placed a long-distance call to Governor Ralston, requesting an "immediate shipment of chloride of lime" and a deployment of the Indiana National Guard's ambulance company to Peru. The governor quickly obliged.[123]

Dr. Cobb also visited the Terre Haute area. He recommended razing Taylorville and condemning it for park purposes, saying:

> *The conditions in Taylorsville* [sic] *may not be expressed in mere words. I have traveled much in every state of the Union…but nowhere have I seen such a menace to the health of its inhabitants, such a menace to the health of a city, such a menace to the health of a state as exists just now at Taylorsville* [sic]. *The entire town should be wiped out of existence.*[124]

A government boat that was tied up at Evansville to administer typhoid and smallpox vaccines to refugee camps displayed a sign: "No vaccination, no rations." At least in some cases, an individual's eligibility to receive federal government aid was contingent on complying with medical recommendations and getting vaccinated.[125]

Once the storms exited, the water receded and attentions turned to flood prevention for the future, the federal government again entered the picture when the task of prevention was beyond state and local capabilities. The U.S. Army Corps of Engineers seemed better positioned to analyze and organize major projects to defeat the uncertainties of weather and water courses. After the corps conducted studies and prepared reports, its plans required the approval of Congress. Finally, financing the approved projects required Congressional appropriations. One looming question was where to find the money. Would local governments or citizens need to share the cost? What economic restrictions would be required in other areas to pay for flood prevention?[126]

CLEANING UP THE MESS

After the water receded, people were faced with the job of cleaning up. City and state officials, engineers and railroad companies tackled the major jobs of rebuilding washed-out railroads, bridges and roads and inspecting and reinforcing damaged infrastructure. Some of the more unique cleanup jobs also needed someone to figure out how best to do them. A log barn near Tunnelton had floated away and was left in the middle of a public highway when the water went down. A house ended up lodged in some trees south of Sparksville, but the residents there did not recognize it. Hoping to find its rightful owner, the news article noted that it was a white house and appeared to be almost new with three rooms. A farmer in Wabash also discovered a house abandoned on his farm after the flood. He was even more surprised when he discovered that the house contained two hundred pounds of dynamite, leaving everyone to wonder where the house had come from and what might have happened if it had struck a bridge on its way down the river.[127]

By the end of the first week, some services had begun to operate again. The March 28 edition of the *Indianapolis News* reported that the Big Four Railroad had resumed its passenger service from Indianapolis to Chicago and hoped to soon have lines open to Terre Haute so that coal could be shipped to Indianapolis. Some of the interurban lines to surrounding cities and towns were working again. The Indianapolis Water Company's Riverside Station pumps had started operating and enough water pressure had been regained to alleviate the fear of having enough water to fight any fires. Telephone service was improving, and the gas supply had improved enough for domestic use.

The ruins of Broadway Street Bridge over Wabash River, circa March 1913. *Miami County Historical Society.*

The damage to North Tenth Street Bridge in Richmond, circa March 1913. *Wayne County Historical Museum.*

Many places did not regain services for a week or more after the flood. The *Bedford Daily Mail* announced on April 1 that the city's steam pump had resumed operation at a reduced capacity. Two feet of mud had settled at the bottom of the pump pit that workers needed to clear before the electric motors could be returned and full capacity reached. Until then, the water pressure was just enough for private consumers and some fire protection—mill operations had to wait. The April 10 edition of the *Columbus Republican* explained the status of the damaged bayou bridge near Edinburgh. The Indianapolis, Columbus & Southern Traction Company could not use the irreparable bridge. Until a new bridge could be built, the traction company planned to transfer passengers at the bayou bridge—as soon as the Flatrock bridge was repaired. After building a temporary bayou bridge, the train could pass, but passengers were required to offload and walk across the temporary bridge and then reload on the other side. It was not known when either the temporary or permanent bayou bridges would be completed. Service on the Big Four line between Columbus and Greensburg was also still awaiting repairs without any word on when that would occur. The April 11 edition of the Newton County *Brook Reporter* noted that trains were still running on a flood schedule, with the through trains unable to go south of Danville because of washed out tracks. The April 16 edition of the *Brookville Democrat* reported that the electric light company had resumed operations for residences and businesses on Monday, April 14, and hoped to have electricity for streetlights the next day. The telephone company, however, was still repairing damaged lines and expected it would "take some time yet to get all of them in working order." The May 2 edition of the *Bedford Daily Mail* discussed the delay in repairing the stone railroad on the Monon between Stone Creek and Harrodsburg. The ballast had been completely washed away, and although extra crews had been pushing to complete the work, it would probably take another week to complete the reballasting. The roadbed on the main line south of Harrodsburg was also still in poor condition, with trains ordered to move slowly over this section.

Meanwhile, relief committees tackled the task of rehabilitating the hundreds of families whose households had been destroyed. In Indianapolis, the committee members started their work on April 1, with a force of volunteers going from house to house in the flooded districts to assess the extent of the damage and the probable needs of each family. The committee employed groups of men to help clean up and repair homes. They started by removing the debris and mud with shovels. Supply stations distributed tubs, mops, shovels, brooms, brushes, pails, washboards and soap to help with

Coffee Street in Indianapolis after the flood, circa 1913. *Indiana Historical Society, P0408.*

the next stage of cleanup. Next, groups of men worked on planing doors, leveling warped floors, mending broken walls, replacing broken siding, repairing furniture and so on.[128]

People wanted to return to their normal lives, and they wanted to clean up the muddy, unhealthy mess the flood left behind. Some civic leaders just wanted the disaster to end so the city could return to normal. Others wanted to exercise caution and ensure that the people living in the flooded areas received information about the health dangers and importance of proper cleaning. The home nursing department of the Indianapolis Civic League planned to give daily instructions to the people of West Indianapolis on the prevention of infectious diseases. Indiana State Board of Health Secretary Dr. John N. Hurty gave a talk at Tomlinson Hall on the prevention of typhoid fever. Other prominent physicians presented daily lessons at schools and churches on how to disinfect homes and prevent infectious diseases.[129]

During the first week of the flood, these differing concerns caused some confusion, with city officials sending contradictory messages to the public. Much to the dismay of the city board of health, Mayor Shank and Superintendent of Police Hyland had removed the barriers to West Indianapolis, permitting residents, local business owners and sightseers to enter the flooded area. The March 28 edition of the *Indianapolis News* reported that Dr. T. Victor Keene, in representing the city board of health

Cleaning up after the flood in Peru, circa March 1913. *Miami County Historical Society.*

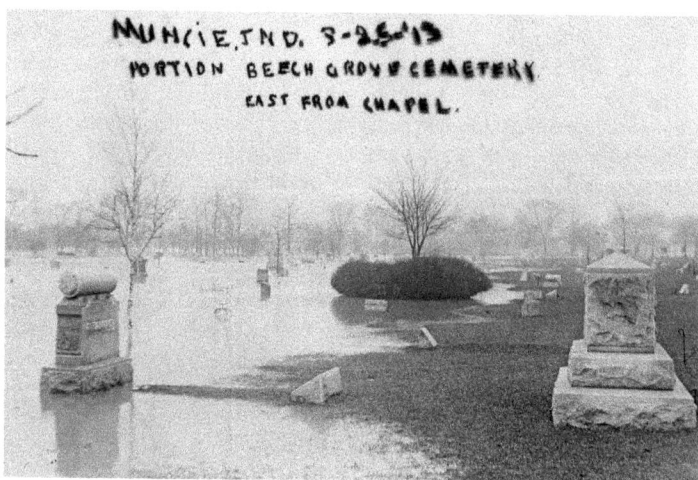

Beech Grove Cemetery (looking east from the chapel) in Muncie, circa March 1913. *Ball State University Archives and Special Collections.*

and working with the general relief committee, had issued a statement: "Allowing free and indiscriminate entry into these homes at this time is a greater calamity than the flood itself." Until the area could be drained of floodwater and homes sanitized, the board of health's position was that the homes, many of which had structural damage, were "absolutely unfit for human habitation." Along with the damaged homes, wells that were used for household water supply had been polluted with floodwater. Dr. Keene, with the support of Dr. Hurty from the state board of health, wanted to issue a restraining order to keep people out of the area. Dr. Hurty also noted the safety concern of preventing widespread fires, as some homeowners had been overheard saying they would have rather had their homes destroyed by fire, which was covered by insurance. Under state law, the city's board had the authority to issue a restraining order due to the "menacing situation," but without cooperation from all city officials, an order could not be enforced.

Typhoid had been a public health concern even before the flood. This bacterial infection, spread through contact with contaminated food or water, caused fever, headache, fatigue, rashes, diarrhea and severe abdominal irritation. If not treated, it could lead to death. Ensuring clean water sources and sanitary food handling was a challenge growing cities faced in the early twentieth century. Although a typhoid vaccine was available in 1913, vaccination was not required or widely practiced. The flood and the conditions left behind raised city officials' concerns about this disease to a new level. Not only had city pumphouses flooded, but so had private wells, and the water supply had intermingled with river and stream pollution, dead animals and all manner of debris. Newspapers printed public service announcements to boil water before drinking, cooking or bathing. Newspapers joined the campaign to inform the public of the dangers lurking in the flood district by publishing statements from public health officials along with photographs and captions aimed at persuading people to honor the quarantine. Boards of health also advised additional precautions like boiling milk, using a coal tar disinfectant in toilets and covering outhouse vaults and garbage with chloride of lime. The Indianapolis Board of Health, fearing an outbreak of typhoid, prepared fifty thousand vials of serum. The state pathology laboratory announced it was administering free typhoid vaccinations at the statehouse and recommended that everyone affected by the current crisis take this protective measure. Private citizens also helped spread the message and encouraged "public desire and sentiment." One man wrote a letter to the editor that was printed in the March 31 edition of the *Indianapolis News*; in the letter, he testified to the efficacy, cost savings and social benefits of vaccination in his own family and quoted a statement from the army medical corps about the 1911 order for compulsory vaccination of soldiers—an indication of a "civilized" army.[130]

RESPONSES, REACTIONS AND EFFECTS

Certainly, communities, neighbors, city officials and charitable organizations were sympathetic to the plight of people who were directly impacted by the flood. The federal government had provided assistance, and the president had sent a message of sympathy and encouragement. After the initial response—and, sometimes, in the midst of the many acts of kindness and charity—the flood initiated other less positive responses, reactions and effects.

For the flood sufferers, cleaning up and recovering from the flood affected their lives on multiple levels, in part because the Great Flood occurred at a crucial time in history. Indiana and many of its cities and towns had been in existence for a century or more. Urban areas had grown in population, and some agrarian towns had changed to urban societies that were reliant on an industrial economy. With these changes came greater demands on the landscape and rivers. Before the 1913 flood, the state, along with the rest of the nation, began to make scientific discoveries that highlighted the connection between the environment and human health. By 1880, scientists had proven the germ theory, and Progressive-Era city administrators had begun to promote clean water and good health as requirements of the modern society. As Suellen Hoy describes in *Chasing Dirt*, "Personal health and comfort forced private individuals to take an interest in their neighbors' sanitary condition." Cleanliness became the national expectation with scientific backing, but "the disturbing possibility lurked that not everyone would share or practice it. Like other features of progressivism, public sanitation and personal cleanliness retained a lingering middle-class, indeed upper middle-class tincture."[131] As communities became attuned to cleanliness, with heightened awareness of the unhealthy conditions of rivers and their tendency to flood, flood control and cleanliness became intertwined and signified progress. Flooding became not only a nuisance but also a fearful, despised occurrence. If a sector of society existed outside of this expected norm, others took note.

Day after day, the headlines and stories in the local newspapers reported on the conditions in West Indianapolis: the dangers of disease, guards posted to prevent anyone who did not live there from entering the area, health advisors sent to counsel on proper cleaning methods, women scooping mud from carpets with shovels, children playing on mud-covered porches and troublesome drainage problems. The caption under a large photograph on the front page of the March 29 edition of the *Indianapolis News* described the scene: "Astor Street on the west side of Indianapolis presented an excellent example of the insanitary conditions that caused the city board of health to take stringent measures in guarding against disease. In the water, which stood in pools, were dead chickens and other animals."[132]

Although flooding had occurred in multiple parts of the capital city, attention focused on West Indianapolis—the "flooded district." City officials combined separate departments—city engineering, the street commissioner and street cleaning, in conjunction with the city board of health—into a temporary department to clean up the flooded district. Several hundred men, divided into fifty teams, converged on the flooded district. They were ordered to first remove all debris and open the sewer manholes to allow the water to drain. They would then begin the work of cleaning up both the inside and outside of the homes. The *Indianapolis News* described the situation in West Indianapolis; residents had spent the night "huddled about little fires in water-soaked homes in almost indescribable insanitary conditions," while city officials "planned methods of saving them from their own folly." Their folly had been to return to their homes—yet they had been permitted to do so by the mayor and superintendent of police.

Because of the flood emergency, the Common Council of Indianapolis introduced a city ordinance on April 16, 1913, that was to become effective immediately, which required daily police inspections to determine whether conditions were dangerous or unsanitary and whether there were any violations of any city ordinance. The ordinance required each police officer to complete daily written reports with a description of the conditions, the name of the offending persons and the names of any witnesses. If the unsanitary premises were not cleaned or the dangers were not removed within five days, the police officers had to file affidavits charging the persons with violations. The police reports were declared to be public records for the use and benefit of the public at large and for the city of Indianapolis.[133]

Labeling flood districts as unclean and inhabitants as criminal was not unique to the capital. The April 16 edition of the *Brookville Democrat* printed a notice from the secretary of the town board of health on the front page: "All property owners are required by law to place their premises in a sanitary condition." It had been three weeks since the flood, and continuing rain had made cleaning difficult, but then, with dry weather, everyone was expected

"Happy Survivors in the Midst of Wreckage after Great Flood," Lawrenceburg, circa March 1913. *Collection of Jenny Awad, Dearborn County State Historian.*

to be cleaning. The town would fumigate properties, but not until property owners had properly cleaned up—that included cleaning cellars and places under the house that could be reached, as "bacteria cannot live in dry sand or nice clean dry earth; it is filth and dampness that they thrive in."

Places that locals had labeled as undesirable prior to the flood received renewed focus after the flood. Taylorville, which was located on the west side of the Wabash River from Terre Haute, was a small community with between seven hundred and one thousand people who were living in poverty-level conditions and had reputations for running into problems with the law. A half-page exposé in the April 12 edition of the *Indianapolis News* described the town's history and then-current state of affairs and called the townspeople a "motley collection of all nationalities," "not afflicted with either thrift or industry" and "the type that live along rivers." The 1913 flood inundated the town, as had floods in the past, but on inspecting the conditions in 1913, the state board of health issued a strict quarantine. Dr. Hurty directed County Health Commissioner Dr. F.W. Shaley to inspect each house and to post a card on any house that was found to be unsanitary with an order for the occupants to move out or face arrest. The townspeople refused to leave their homes, calling the evacuation order "medical tyranny." The *Indianapolis News* noted, "They had lived in squalor for years and were willing to continue to live the same way—they did not fear disease." In fairness, Dr. Hurty noted Terre Haute's contribution to the conditions in Taylorville. Part of the town was situated on land used for the city dump, and the city had allowed people to dump "all kinds of decayed vegetable and animal matter there, contrary to all requirements of the health laws." Dr. Hurty recommended soaking the dump with gas and setting fire to it. He also recommended condemning the town and turning the land into a park. The town was labeled as "unwanted" after the park commissioners declined the suggestion and Terre Haute refused to annex the town.[134]

Negative labeling following the 1913 flood further separated the flooded area from the rest of the city. The *Indianapolis News* reported, "Many of them had lost what to them was a great deal. There are days of discomfort and work ahead of them, but the end of the flood and the opportunity of getting back home was a happy incident, and more than one whistled as he started the work of cleaning house." Certainly, West Indianapolis residents wanted to get back home and back to work, but the task of doing so was overwhelming. As the news delivered messages that this area was unclean and unfit, it also reported that the West Indianapolis residents had happily moved back without regard to the health risks.[135] The flood sufferers were not only labeled as victims of a disaster but also as people living in unhealthy conditions, which had long-lasting effects. Prior to the flood, the property values of homes in the West Indianapolis "valley" were lower than homes on the "hill." Flooding highlighted this difference and entrenched the valley in a negative identity. One West Indianapolis resident who was interviewed in the 1970s said, "When I was young, eyebrows would be raised if a girl or boy from the 'hill' dated someone from the 'valley.'"[136]

While the Great Flood was happening, other unfortunate events occurred. Some people saw opportunities for their own advancement during this time of crisis, requiring police and militia to turn their attention from rescue and aid missions to fighting crime. In Indianapolis, police were instructed to watch out for plunderers, with reported orders to "shoot on sight" anyone caught in the act. The police department established a lockdown of the flooded area, closely monitoring anyone leaving or entering, and they had closed down the saloons, presumably to help everyone stay on task. Governor Ralston prepared a proclamation of martial law to control vandalism and robbery in the flooded district of Indianapolis but decided not to take that drastic step. Although the governor did not issue the formal proclamation, he ordered two companies of the Indiana National Guard to patrol West Indianapolis, with other companies placed on call.[137]

The capital was not the only city facing this problem. After receiving a report that "a large number of suspicious characters had made their appearance" in Logansport, the governor ordered another company of national guardsmen to that city. The Cass County Sheriff Department had sworn in three hundred deputies, but the militia would help ward off lawlessness.[138] In Muncie, national guardsmen reported chasing away men who were trying to enter flood-bound homes on North Jefferson and Elm Streets. After folks in the Evansville suburb of Oakdale had to evacuate their homes, looters succeeded in entering and stealing personal property. Police officers took on the additional task of patrolling neighborhoods to prevent this atrocity from continuing.[139]

The relief committee in Indianapolis received word that "loan sharks" had set up offices in the flooded district, preying on those in need. Apparently, the loan sharks befriended flood victims, offered to loan them money to get back on their feet and charged exorbitant interest rates. The relief committee posted warning signs in the flood district noting that trusted loans could be obtained from the public welfare association established by Indianapolis citizens.[140]

Other manifestations of greed came in the form of price gouging. With food items like bread, butter, milk, eggs, meat and coffee in short supply, some vendors began raising their prices. In Indianapolis, the police superintendent instructed his officers to investigate and immediately arrest any merchants or restaurant owners who had increased prices, and a grand jury was called to investigate those individuals accused of taking advantage of the crisis in this way. One report that reached the criminal court judge was of a dealer who charged a little girl twenty-five cents for a loaf of rye bread. The president of Taggart Baking Company, speaking on behalf of local bakeries, denied that they had raised their wholesale prices from the pre-flood price of four cents a loaf, but he had heard that some retailers had inflated their prices to as much as thirty-five cents a loaf after the flood. The governor again threatened martial law, stating that he "would raise the devil with anyone" who tried "to make money out of misfortune."[141]

Still others took advantage of the charity that was extended by fellow community members or of the situation in general. Relief committees learned to recognize these cases to avoid the loss of invaluable provisions to these imposters. It seemed that the people who were in actual distress were hesitant to ask for assistance, as compared to those who were not.[142] The March 28 edition of the *Fort Wayne Sentinel* told of the "meanest man in town," who had been assisting rescuers, but stole one dollar of relief money that had been given to him to buy coal oil and bread for a marooned family. The evidence against him was "conclusive" when the grocer called to verify that the man was authorized to charge the city for the items. The man was charged with petty larceny for his deed. Whether he was the meanest man was questionable, however, as another man was running a similar scam at the Wells Street bridge. He, too, was caught in the act and sentenced to sixty days in jail. It was believed that the two men were in town for the express purpose of looting.

THE SPECTACLE OF THE FLOOD

Floods of this magnitude did not happen often, and the 1913 flood raised the curiosity of many. In Indianapolis, an estimated twenty thousand people gathered to witness White River win its battle against the West Washington Street bridge, despite the dangerous situation. Policemen were stationed at each end to keep people off the bridge and "were forced to fight to keep back the spectators." About two thousand people watched and waited for the impending collapse of the twenty-five-foot levee holding back White River along Morris Street. The break began as a tiny stream around 3:00 p.m. on Tuesday, March 25, until it broke at 6:10 p.m., flooding the working-class neighborhood of West Indianapolis. Spectators watched as the first break occurred at 4:00 p.m., and water began to enter homes. They watched as people waded through the water, carrying sacks, suitcases, baskets of food, pictures and other personal belongings. Some had wagons filled with furniture and stoves, while others hauled pens of chickens, but they all rushed toward the Morris Street bridge to escape the flood. The spectators watched as the water reached the top of the levee but were awestruck when, instead of cutting through the top, the water burst through the bottom of the levee. Tons of rock caved in and a twenty-five-foot-tall wall of water that was a half-mile wide rushed through the levee. Any hope of saving the homes disappeared. As noted by an *Indianapolis Star* reporter, the catastrophe "meant, in many cases, the sacrifice of savings of a lifetime."[143]

When Mayor Shank and Police Superintendent Hyland removed the bars to allow entry into the flood district on March 28, sightseers came to "view the ruins." The April 3 edition of the *Hancock Democrat* reported that a number of people from that neighboring county had taken a sightseeing trip to Indianapolis on Saturday, March 29.

By Sunday, March 30, the floodwaters had receded enough in many locations to allow people to safely leave their homes and see the devastation for themselves. A Sunday seemed to be a good day for an outing. A *Martinsville Reporter-Times* reporter joined a group that was traveling by car to Waverly to "view the wreckage." They were not alone, as many others also traveled from miles around by buggy, automobile and horseback. Many families brought a picnic dinner with them, and he compared the sight to "an old-time camp meeting," with "vehicles hitched to every available space near the town." The spectators were not disappointed, as the wreckage of homes, businesses, bridges and streets came into view as soon as the road turned into Waverly. For those who could not make the trip, the printed article described some of the sights: a home sitting halfway in water, with the other half on crumbling ground; a barn washed two blocks away and standing on someone else's farm; and household articles strewn along the road and standing in fields, including parts of beds, a wash stand, a clock and a hat rack.[144]

The crowds of people who were flocking to the flooded districts prompted one Englewood family to tabulate the number of those passing by on Mitchell Pike. As reported in the *Bedford Daily Mail* on Monday, March 31, between Thursday and Sunday, they watched and counted 1,304 people walking, 500 buggies and carriages, 414 autos and hacks, 238 motors and bicycles, 53 wagons and 20 people on horseback. Friday and Sunday were the most popular days for these outings.

The same phenomenon occurred in Evansville once the worst of the flooding occurred there. The Monday, April 7 edition of the *Evansville Press* reported that, on Sunday, seventy thousand curious people had flocked to marvel at the heights of the Ohio River and the flooded neighborhoods. A stream of pedestrians walked along the riverfront and to the Oakdale and Linwood Avenue sections of the city. Some even "gondoliered through the fashionable, asphalted, tree-fringed streets." Green River streetcars posted signs on the front, saying, "This way to the flooded district," and they departed with passengers every few minutes. The streetcars had a profitable day, with a reported twenty thousand riders, about one-fourth of Evansville's population. Evansville's real estate agents also took advantage of this opportunity to promote the lots that were situated above the floodwater level to prospective buyers—an especially effective visual in comparison to the lots that were underwater.

MISCELLANY

The flood had far-reaching effects and impacted businesses and events in some unexpected ways. Mentions of the flood continued to appear in newspapers in the following weeks and months.

Workers at the American Sheet and Tin Plate Company in Elwood did not receive their March 29 paychecks because the flood conditions prevented the train that was carrying those paychecks from arriving from the company's eastern offices. The teachers' examinations, which were scheduled for Saturday, March 29, in Mitchell, were delayed until the following Saturday because the questions failed to arrive from Indianapolis. Indiana University president William L. Bryan postponed resuming the semester after spring break because railroads remained incapacitated and students could not return to school. The Brookville librarian posted a notice in the paper asking anyone who had lost a library book in the flood to report the title at the library desk, including overdue books. The April 9 edition of the *Brookville Democrat* also posted that the library would be open from 2:00 p.m. to 5:00 p.m. daily until electricity was restored, at which time, evening hours could be resumed.[145]

The baseball season was delayed; although, in some places, that was not unusual. The owner of Fort Wayne's baseball park said he would wait until the flood was over before assessing the damage and taking another chance on fixing up the place. Apparently, since he had bought the baseball franchise, the park had flooded every spring except for one. The damage in 1913 was expected to be greater than it had been in previous years, but he seemed to take it in stride. After all, the city had more important issues to focus on, and contractors had more urgent work to complete.[146]

A young couple who had been married on April 2 in Evansville had to delay their plans to move to their new home in St. Louis, Missouri, until flood conditions would permit travelling. In the meantime, they returned to stay with friends who lived in a flooded neighborhood. The newlyweds, dressed in their wedding finery, were carried through the water from a cab to a boat to be ferried to their friends' home.[147]

The April 3 edition of the *Columbus Republican* reported on an unusual famine that was affecting Bartholomew County—a shovel famine. Regardless of whether they were long-handled, short-handled, pointed, rounded, flat, big or little, shovels were in high demand, and stores were sold out. Railroad companies were hiring anyone who needed a job to help repair the lines, and shovels were needed to do the job. Farmers were also in need of shovels, as they were working to repair country roads. The April 16 edition of the *Brookville Democrat* posted a notice asking for rubber boots. The relief committee had furnished volunteers with boots during the initial relief and cleanup effort, and their supply had been depleted. With a continuing need for rubber boots for ongoing cleanup, the committee asked anyone who was no longer using their boots to return them. The committee had also received requests to buy boots, so if boots were returned, the proceeds from sold boots could be deposited in the relief fund.

Newspapers published advertisements for photographs that had been taken of the flood available for reasonable prices. These enterprises promoted their "first-class negatives" and quality photographs or postcards of the flood destruction. Other businesses utilized the flood as a way to promote goods and services. A local bank placed an advertisement in the *Brookville Democrat* with a title in bold type: "The Flood." The bank advertised its role in helping the afflicted get back into their homes and noted that funds placed in its care would be safe from thieves, floods and fire. A real estate office ran its advertisement in the *Fort Wayne Gazette* with the eye-catching title, "A Great Flood of Business," promoting its abundant listings of farms, lots and homes with terms to suit purchasers. A home furnishings store posted an advertisement in the *Fort Wayne Sentinel* directed specifically toward flood victims about "a number of big specials in our rug and lace curtain departments," noting, "We want to save you money." Another home furnishings store ran its advertisement in the April 7 edition of the *Evansville Press* before the floodwaters began to recede; it announced its "April shower of bargains" with "a flood of values" on rugs.[148]

The Webb Dry Goods Company advertised its annual anniversary sale in the May 20 edition of the *Bedford Daily Mail*. Because of flood delays, shipments from Onyx Hosiery had not arrived in time for their usual sale on hosiery in mid-April; instead, the advertisement stated, "We propose to use them to swell the crowd this anniversary sale." The arrival of summer knit underwear and children's dresses had also been delayed by the flood, but these items had arrived in time for this sale and would be available for "special prices."

Cartoonists turned their attentions to the events surrounding the flood; some searched for humor in the situation, some took a satirical approach and others served as public service announcements. With concerns about the spread of disease in the weeks after the flood, the April 3 edition of the *Indianapolis News* printed a cartoon that showed a character wearing a hat labeled "Public" worriedly swatting at a bug with the caption: "And don't forget to boil the water for drinking and for domestic purposes."

In the midst of the flood, some Indiana cities proceeded with scheduled elections to decide whether or not they would permit saloons to sell intoxicating beverages—to go "dry" or "wet." This highly contested issue spurred many voters to brave the conditions to cast their ballot. Delphi held its vote on Tuesday, with many voters transported to the polls by boat. The drys won the vote in Delphi by 162 votes, increasing their winning margin from two years earlier. Columbia City held its election on Wednesday, and the drys won with 322 votes as compared to 312 wets. Voters had to take a boat across the river to reach the voting place, with each side having its own ferry line. Before either line would take a passenger, they had to declare their vote. In Princeton, an estimated 90 percent of folks braved the flood conditions on April 2, with close results—829 drys and 781 wets. The flood did not seem to sway voters to go wet. Officials in other cities and towns decided to defer their elections until late April, and at least in some cases, the wets won. After being dry for two years, on April 28, Laurel's wet voters won the election by a majority of 16 votes.[149]

Property taxes came due on May 15, based on the assessed value of property on March 1. Because of the flood, the State Board of Tax Commissioners issued a notice in mid-April, reminding all local assessment officers of the procedures outlined in state law. If unavoidable casualty loss occurred after March 1, the date the property value was determined, the property owner could file a sworn proof of loss, with the county auditor receiving a rebate. If the loss was covered by insurance, the property owner would not be eligible for a rebate; however, because flood insurance was not available, property owners would be eligible. The state board requested that this information be widely publicized. Flood sufferers needed to be aware of these procedures, pay their property taxes and then file an affidavit to receive a rebate.[150]

A farmer near Flat Rock discovered that the flood had uncovered a Native American burial ground on his property. The skeletons of an adult and a child were found with hatchets, pipes and other artifacts nearby. On further investigation, more skeletons were found, along with campfire circles, pottery, arrow heads and lead bullets. A physician examined the skeletons and believed they belonged to members of the Flathead Tribe. Unfortunately, the farmer had to post signs to stop visitors from collecting souvenirs.[151]

A great number of seagulls were spotted flying over the high water in Muncie. It was the first time the birds had been seen in Delaware County, and it was presumed that they were attracted down to the flooded area from the large lakes to the north.[152]

4.

LESSONS OF THE FLOOD

L ong before the 1913 flood, people had begun solving the mysteries of flooding and had noticed the connection between the rivers, the weather and human action. American scholars wrote about the importance of the human relationship with nature as early as 1864, when George P. Marsh introduced his book *The Earth as Modified By Human Action*, in which he pointed to the connection between settlement patterns, such as deforestation, and increased flooding, erosion and climate changes. Marsh had advocated for keeping humans away from the rivers in the mid-nineteenth century, and his advice again entered conversations after the 1913 flood.

Understanding Rivers, Floodplains, Weather and Disasters

In 1913, recording the weather had been an interest for both scientists and citizens. After all, if humans could record the weather and study it, maybe they could understand it and predict it. In 1849, the Smithsonian Institute provided weather instruments to a network of telegraph offices, where volunteers could report their observations. In 1870, U.S. military stations began recording meteorological observations by magnetic telegraph and marine signals for the benefit of commerce. The U.S. Weather Bureau came into existence in 1891, after President Benjamin Harrison recommended changing the agency from a meteorological division of the federal government's War Department to a civilian service under the Department of Agriculture, and the Weather Bureau was made responsible for issuing flood warnings to the public via telegraph. Data from twenty-six stations on the Mississippi River and its tributaries supplied the information. The practice of recording river levels also became widespread in cities and towns across the country in the 1880s. In the late 1800s and early 1900s, however, weather science was rudimentary by today's standards, whether it was observed by the U.S. Weather Bureau or by local volunteers.[153]

Explanations of what happened in 1913 appeared in newspapers following the flood. Perhaps people needed assurance that the disaster could be explained. Apart from weather science, other disciplines and experts in their field contributed their opinions. The March 27 edition of the *Fort Wayne Sentinel* printed an article written by Albert Ford Ferguson, who sought to answer a troubling question: "Why is it that great walls of water annually hurl themselves through the Ohio Valley or the Mississippi Valley?" Ferguson answered this question with a lesson in the topography of the United States from the time of its formation. As he explained it, with an accompanying map, a ridge running across the northern parts of Illinois, Indiana and Ohio is the dividing point that causes rain or snowmelt to flow either southwesterly to the Mississippi or north to the Great Lakes. The formation of the sloped landscape south of the ridge left Indiana and Ohio—where the worst of the flood had occurred—at the lowest part of the central plain and at the "natural outlet for all the excess moisture of a vast region."

Yet two floods in Fort Wayne in 1873 and 1877 had demonstrated the significance of the combination of variables that influence flooding. In April 1873, all three rivers overflowed their banks at the same time and flooded the north side with so much water that only the roofs of houses and the treetops were visible. In April 1877, the snow thaws occurred at different times, and the St. Mary's River overflowed two weeks earlier than the St. Joseph's River. When only one river overflowed, Fort Wayne residents noticed the different flood impact. With these floods in the 1870s, concerns about flooding had changed focus—the threat to modern infrastructure, like bridges and railroads, rose to the top of residents' lists of concerns when flooding occurred.[154]

The April 3 edition of the *Bedford Daily Mail* printed an article cautioning engineers and architects to remember that old flood marks are "not necessarily conclusive." Floodwaters would naturally not have risen as rapidly or to the high levels seen in more modern floods because the state had been heavily forested in the past. The article noted that the severity of floods had been increasing in recent times, and despite being "intelligently governed," the 1913 flood proved that cities and towns could be "unexpectedly and deeply submerged."

An editorial printed in the March 25 edition of the *South Bend Tribune* called the "awful havoc of the storms dreadful but not stupefying." Touting human dominion over the earth, its creatures and the oceans, the author of the article claimed that humans knew more then than they ever had before and were becoming better prepared in understanding meteorological conditions and providing advance notice—"It is but occasionally that such a disaster as that of Sunday occurs." Taking his positivity further, the author claimed, "The killed are heroic sacrifices to the advanced knowledge of men." And he noted, "Because they have died, mankind will be only the more determined to provide against future calamities." Others agreed—at least they agreed that the wisdom gained would be applied to future buildings and that engineering skill would prevent a travesty like this one from happening again.

Still others looked for the teachable moments that were offered by the flood. During Reverend A.J. Folsom's sermon at the Plymouth Congregational Church on Sunday, March 30, he spoke about the benefits of the disaster: raising awareness of the "sacredness of home"; making friends dearer than ever, whether old or new; and awakening sympathy and making the maxim "to love one another" a reality. He called for extending these benefits throughout the year, not just in a time of disaster. The reverend also addressed the matter of blame and the human tendency to seek someone or something to blame. He urged the congregation to blame neither God nor the city administrators but to instead "use good sense and see the very practical truth of the whole matter…the lesson of the frailty of the works of man." He called the forces of nature our "best friends" and noted that "as intelligent beings," people have known of the precarious relationship with the rivers and landscape.[155]

THE HUMAN RELATIONSHIP WITH RIVERS AND LANDSCAPE

While ideas about the cause of the flood and the lessons learned varied widely, the 1913 flood raised serious questions and prompted discussions about what could be done to prevent future floods. Part of those discussions focused on the effects of modernizing cities. Opinions about what would work to prevent future floods were plentiful. Many places turned their attentions toward the river and asked what modifications could be made to change the river's behavior. *Would bigger and stronger levees prevent flooding in the future? Would straightening bends in the river help? Would installing cement banks keep the river from departing from its course? Could a dam and a reservoir provide a more modern way to monitor and control the river?*

This national calamity, as President Wilson called it, raised two additional questions: Who should be responsible for flood prevention—the federal government or each state—and who would pay for it? However, this was not the first time that the question of federal or state authority over flood control had risen to the national level and gone before Congress. One important point of contention was whether the federal government had the right to impose a national system on states and overrule each state's right to handle flood control as it saw fit. Advocates in favor of federal intervention argued that any effective method of flood control required a broad and comprehensive approach. Rivers and their floodplains did not restrict themselves to one state and flood control plans shouldn't either. Any navigable river was considered, under long-standing law, to be an interstate highway and fell under federal jurisdiction. The federal government could deploy the U.S. Army Corps of Engineers to study, plan and implement a project of this scale. Advocates for state control noted that many of the flooded rivers were not navigable rivers under federal control and that states were in a better position to know what would work best in their particular situation. After all, each state's geography, climate, culture and history were unique. This philosophical divide seemed insurmountable and unending. Could a compromise be reached in order to resolve the important issue of flood control?[156]

Then there was the question of cost. A flood control project of the anticipated scale—with dams, reservoirs, levees, drainage channels and river modifications—would cost millions of dollars. Flood control advocates acknowledged the incredible costs associated with these projects, but they asked what the costs of human lives and the well-being of those who lived in flood-prone areas were. *Shouldn't the human side of the equation outweigh the monetary cost of flood control?* Other experts believed that the flood control projects would pay for themselves by avoiding the high costs of flood damage and by generating income. In 1907, U.S. Chief Hydrographer M.E. Leighton proposed a system of reservoirs to control flooding in the Mississippi and Ohio River Valleys. Although the estimated cost to build was between $125 and $250 million, Leighton claimed the system would pay for itself, as it would not only prevent floods (and the associated damages), but it would also generate sixty million horsepower of energy.[157]

While this debate continued at the state and federal level, the affected cities and towns were left to face the specter of future floods. At the local level, meetings and planning commenced, but those discussions were also rife with debate about what should be done, how it would be done and who would benefit. Part of deciding what needed to be done for the future depended on knowing what had been done before. The effectiveness of those prior actions necessarily entered these discussions.

In Indianapolis, the city engineer recommended straightening and widening White River and building levees and roadways on both banks. He convinced the board of public works that this work would permanently prevent floods like the one the area had just experienced from happening again. Although he did not yet have an estimate of the cost for the project, the board's resolution provided that it would be paid for by a combination of a municipal bond issue and a tax assessment paid by the property owners who would benefit from the project. During the course of several meetings that were held the week after the flood and attended by public works and park board members and a delegation of west side residents, the proposed plan and issues were discussed at length. The city engineer shared his research on the history of the river. He explained that the reason the levees had been in ill repair could be explained by a conflict of authority rising out of the 1787 Northwest Ordinance that held White River was a navigable stream and an 1876 Indiana Supreme Court decision that held it was not. Whether the river was navigable was important because its status determined who owned and was responsible for not only the banks but the property extending to the center of the stream. As a non-navigable stream, its ownership was divided among each of the property owners. An attorney in attendance proposed that if the river were ruled navigable, the city could ask the federal government for assistance with building the levees. Congressman Charles A. Korbly pointed out that involving the federal government would delay matters. The group agreed that the levee work should proceed under authority of state drainage laws.[158]

Repairing levees and bridges in Indianapolis was underway by the end of the week after the flood, and the city engineer explained the work in progress. Delays had occurred because the crippled railways had made it difficult to get supplies to Indianapolis. The plans to build a temporary bridge over White River at Washington Street was one of those delayed projects. Delays in the city's progress toward flood prevention continued for numerous reasons. On the first anniversary of the flood, the *Indianapolis News* ran an article about the historic flood, including photographs from then and one year later. One year later, the Washington Street bridge had still not been repaired, leaving the West Indianapolis flood district stranded on the other side of the river.[159]

Making repairs was only the beginning. What the city needed was a comprehensive plan for flood control, which the city engineer explained would first require a survey, planning, authorization and funding. To say that the task before the city was "big" was an understatement. Multiple areas of the city had been flooded, and the multiple streams running through the city necessitated a coordinated plan to prevent future floods. As the meeting continued with grievances aired, some pointed out the city's inequities. A local reverend guessed that Fall Creek would be repaired before West Indianapolis, and he said he had already seen that the Big Four track repairs were completed with trains running again, although little attention had been given to the broken levee. Referencing Progressive-Era ideals, he said, "You can talk about a city beautiful until you are sick and crazy about it, but it is a city beautiful at the expense of five thousand of your citizens." Some West Indianapolis residents at the meeting wanted a seawall built to protect the area, pointing out that "there are a lot of men over there buying their own property." Many felt that receiving an old shirt or some furniture would not help them make repairs to the houses they were buying—not when they had to build a new foundation, put in new plastering and hang new wallpaper. They needed protection. One resident testified that, although all his personal property had been ruined in the flood, he was "'hanging on' to West Indianapolis because he had partly paid for his home." Senator Henry Harmon asked for immediate protection for West Indianapolis and called it criminal to expect a resident to return there without protection when "a rise of five feet of the river would cause him to be drowned in his bed." City Councilman Copeland assured the attendees that he would not vote in favor of the proposed $150,000 bond issue unless he had assurance that "a good part of it would go to West Indianapolis to build up the levees."[160]

In Fort Wayne, community members gathered on Monday, March 31, to discuss how another flood of this magnitude could be avoided in the future. The board of park commissioners asked Civil Engineer A.W. Grosvenor to survey and draw a topographical map of the St. Mary's, St. Joseph's and Maumee Rivers' paths through the city. Grosvenor obliged and presented his map and recommendations, which were printed in the April 3 edition of the *Fort Wayne Sentinel*. The article outlined Grosvenor's overarching message: remove

After flood had receded.

WASHINGTON ST. BRIDGE FROM WEST SIDE INDIANAPOLIS, MAR 1913.

Washington Street Bridge from the west side after the flood had receded, circa March 1913. *Indiana Historical Society, P0326.*

obstructions to the rivers' flow, including trash, soil and sand buildup, dirt dumped from excavations, street sweepings, cinders and ashes and human-built encroachments (e.g., walls, bridges, buildings). Specifically, he recommended an in-depth survey of the rivers; dredging and removing high points in the river channels; cutting a cross section through the city for the St. Mary's River, which would include removing anything built in its path; redirecting the St. Mary's River with a gradual turn into the Maumee River; increasing the size of the river channels and removing obstructions; raising St. Joe Boulevard and the Lakeside Dike; and, if those steps did not prevent flooding, extending the Trier Ditch and connecting the St. Mary's River with the Maumee River south of the city. Following that initial survey and meeting, the community members formed a flood prevention committee, which included prominent citizens and nine engineers, to continue studying the problems and recommend changes. The *Sentinel* promised that the April 3 article would be the first in a series of articles aimed at keeping the public informed. Two years later, Mayor William J. Hosey and the city council approved the committee's recommendations, and the work of re-engineering the rivers began.[161]

Fort Wayne's quick response and progress on future prevention may relate in part to attempts that had been made in the past to take similar action. The March 31 edition of the *Sentinel* included a letter to the editor calling the readers' attention to the 1912 proposal for a $200,000 bond issue for river improvements, which, if approved, would have included dredging the channel, elevating the river banks and controlling floodwaters and likely would have avoided this disaster. The writer continued by suggesting that those who had opposed that bond issue "under the leadership" of Mayor Hosey "have much to answer for." The 1912 proposal was defeated in part because of the associated tax increase. "Now," he claimed, "we have paid a heavy penalty for following Hosey's advice." It took a disaster with estimated damages of $850,000 to make clear the necessity of these improvements, leaving the city in a worse position and still in need of those improvements.[162]

Discussions about the different possibilities for flood control began in Muncie the same week the flood occurred. One prominent citizen advocated for digging a new, straightened river channel to divert White River from the city. He had studied the problem and suggested a straight cut from the Whitley bridge to Yorktown, where a natural depression occurred. This approach would take Muncie out of the flood zone, saving the city from costly flood damage in the future. It would be expensive to complete the project, but he believed the benefits outweighed the costs and would save money in the long run. Noting that the promises made after the 1904 flood—that reinforcing the levees would prevent future problems—had proved inaccurate, he wanted to abandon the levee approach. He had also researched the city's original plans. Apparently, a city pioneer named Goldsmith Gilbert had a similar idea, and sometime in the mid- to late 1800s, Gilbert had plowed furrows in the vicinity of the Whitley bridge to prevent high water, redirecting the river several hundred feet farther away from the courthouse. In 1913, this citizen thought it was time to again adjust the river's path.[163]

In Evansville, the city engineer received approval to begin the process of preventing one significant impact of flooding while the city was still in the throes of the flood. On April 2, a notice appeared in the *Evansville Press* informing property owners in the neighborhood that were served by the Kentucky Avenue sewer that floodgates and pumps would be installed to fix the backed-up sewers as soon as the floodwater receded. For these residents, flooding had not been a problem until the city installed the sewer line.[164]

The Brookville Commercial Club held its regular meeting on April 11, and its discussions included matters of the city's "future prosperity." Attendees agreed that the valley section of town needed protection from future floods, and they appointed a committee to "consider plans" and "confer with the county commissioners" at their next meeting. Plans to obtain federal assistance with protection were underway as well. U.S. Vice President Thomas R. Marshall (from North Manchester, Indiana) had personally asked the secretary of war to send an engineer to Brookville to advise the town on how to make repairs and insure against future floods. Although the secretary responded that he was swamped with such requests, he would do his best. In the meantime, the Franklin County surveyor began taking measurements and preparing a survey in anticipation of the arrival of a government engineer.[165]

Officials, experts and residents in every city and town impacted by the flood presumably turned their thoughts toward ways to prevent a similar disaster in the future. Their thoughts also likely turned to ways in which communities could become better prepared for future floods. Muncie's sheriff again raised the recommendation, which had previously been raised in 1904, that the town purchase motorboats. He claimed that a marine lifesaving station near the High Street bridge would have made rescue work more efficient and less dangerous. As it was, rescues had to be conducted on horseback, using treacherous flatboats or canoes or by carrying people out of the water when possible. The sheriff had firsthand experience with these antiquated methods, as a swift current had capsized his boat while he was trying to rescue women and children, tossing everyone on board into the water.[166]

The flood showcased the limitations of the existing communication systems in America. Depending on wires strung along poles had proved to be a handicap during a disaster and a source of frustration in Washington, D.C. Without the ability to receive information from the flood-stricken areas, the president and federal agencies had no way of knowing exactly what assistance was needed. As it was, the president had to dispatch the secretary of war to the flooded areas, and he then had to report back. Without traveling there through treacherous conditions, citizens were left in the dark as to the fate of their family and friends in other towns. Likewise, business owners could not receive information about the status of their concerns. Wireless telegraphy was available in 1913, but its use had been restricted to private enterprises, which opposed government intervention in the industry. Establishing a government-run wireless system for emergency purposes seemed cost prohibitive, except when compared to the government's expenditures to maintain an army and navy in preparation for war. It came down to a matter of profits—at the time, wired lines of communication generated profits, but wireless systems did not. If the government were to establish a wireless communication system that would be available for both government and commercial use, private industry would be left out of the profits. To many, this dilemma highlighted the big business priorities of profits over the protection of human lives. At a time when the country was attuned to preventing another tragedy like the Great Flood, those of the mindset that the government should provide protection to citizens pointed out that the existing communication system under corporate control held people captive to corporate profits. The question presented to Wilson's administration was whether the federal government would acquire and maintain all wireless telegraphy for the good of the country.[167]

Some raised the question of whether flood insurance could be purchased. The April 1 edition of the *Indianapolis News* included a short letter from the Western Underwriter stating that it had received "numerous letters" asking if any company wrote flood insurance, but unfortunately, no company did. The possibility of flood insurance had been discussed in the past, however. Just the year before, the paper had published articles from an insurance agent in Iowa who had devised such a "scheme." The agent had not been able to convince any company to take up the risky business of flood insurance.

Highlighting the wide range of proposed solutions and the complicated human relationship with rivers, the front page of the April 9 edition of the *Evansville Press* included a long article titled "Join the Smile Club." Filled with optimism, witty quips and a lighthearted poem, the article delivered the message that the people of Evansville had "no reason whatever to worry" about the flood. Businessmen did not need to frown, as soon, neighbors would be back on their feet and coming to Evansville—to buy. Encouraging everyone to have a positive attitude, pull together and see what could be done, the author suggested, "By the first of May, we will have forgotten all about the flood." His solution was, "Make up your mind that 1913 will be your best year."

LATER FLOOD EVENTS

Despite a greater understanding of the nature of rivers, plans to take action to prevent future floods and plans to implement improved protective measures, floods continued to visit Indiana's cities and towns, some with devastating effects. Indeed, flooding in Indiana is inevitable; the water has to go somewhere.

In Fort Wayne, the methodical study and extensive actions taken to prevent future flood disasters seemed to work for about thirty years. When the rivers left their banks and spread across the city in 1943, the weather conditions were not as severe—without the high winds and frigid temperatures of 1913—and the city seemed to take it in stride. Comparing this event to the Great Flood no doubt helped put it in perspective. Major floods occurred again in 1959 and 1978, but the March 1982 flood rivaled the 1913 flood, coming within two-tenths of a foot of the earlier flood's high level. Some of the same areas of the city flooded again in 1982, but there were differences, too. The 1982 flood occurred suddenly during the night, and it was restricted to Fort Wayne, unlike the Great Flood. Regardless, the 1982 flood caused $56.1 million in damage. The city again launched a campaign to prevent future floods, working with the U.S. Army Corps of Engineers and spending $50 million on measures that took nineteen years to complete and included over ten miles of new or enhanced dikes. In the summer of 2001, the same year the projects were completed, another flood occurred. This one occurred in the southern part of Fort Wayne, flooding areas that were not protected by the new dikes and causing $10.6 million in damage. Since 2001, the city has continued to fight against destructive floods and has continued to experience floods.[168]

In Evansville, the 1913 flood had failed to surpass the 1884 flood by a mere five inches. The 1884 historic crest at 48.82 feet, however, paled in comparison to the January 1937 crest at 53.75 feet. Evansville considers the 1937 flood as the most devastating, as do other cities located near the Ohio River. In 1937, 90 percent of the town of Jeffersonville flooded. The small town of Leavenworth, which had settled along the banks of the Ohio River, relocated to the bluffs behind its original location following the 1937 flood. New Deal advocates "questioned the logic of spending billions" to construct flood control projects for communities located on the banks of the Ohio River. Relocating communities, with the aid of the Civilian Conservation Corps, seemed more logical; although, others viewed this option as a "defeatist ideology." Many of Leavenworth's residents opposed the move, and some refused to leave, but eventually, the town did relocate.[169]

In 1993, a massive region-wide flood event occurred over a six-month period, affecting portions of eight midwestern states, displacing more than 100,000 people and resulting in damage that was estimated to cost as much as $20 billion. Calling the 1993 flood "just one of the many that have been seen before and will be seen again," an Interagency Floodplain Management Review Committee prepared a report titled "Sharing the Challenge," in which it noted that the "United States simply has lacked the focus and incentive to engage itself seriously in floodplain management."

The 1937 high-water mark on the second story of a building in Leavenworth. Note the 1913 flood mark on first-story door. The town relocated after the 1937 flood. *Indiana Historical Society.*

Although the federal government could set an example, the committee emphasized that "state and local governments must manage their own floodplains" and that individuals "must adjust their actions to the risks they face and bear a greater share of the economic costs." Widespread flooding occurred again in 2008, affecting eleven midwestern states. The U.S. Geological Survey reported that Indiana endured the most recurrent flooding in 2008, with "peak-of-record stream flows" in the months of January, February, March, June and September. When two to ten inches of rain fell on central and southern Indiana between June 7 and June 9, 2008, after experiencing high spring rainfall, thirty-nine Indiana counties were declared federal disaster areas. As one example of the severe damage, Indiana's Columbus Regional Hospital incurred $125 million in damage. Overall, the 2008 flood claimed the lives of eleven people and caused damage in excess of $5 billion. Major flooding occurred again in the Midwest in 2011, 2013, 2015, 2016, 2017 and 2019.[170]

Indiana residents have continued to experience major flooding in the twenty-first century. More surprising than that, however, is that flood events have continued to surprise Indiana residents. Although there were many lessons to learn from earlier floods and science and technology advanced tremendously after 1913, the fact remains that Hoosiers settled on a flood-prone landscape.

The Great Flood of 1913 gained its name in part because that name was broadly published and used at the time. But the event was worthy of the name not only because of the devastation caused and the records it set, but also because of the attention it brought to the problem of flooding in Indiana. It drew attention to this eternal natural phenomenon and the dangerous limits it imposed on modernity, including the hopes and dreams of people who sought economic growth and progress. Perhaps calling it the Great Flood suggested that it was an unusual event that would not happen again, at least not during the lifetimes of those who experienced it. The story of the 1913 flood has been lost in history many times, although it is dusted off and reappears in the news when other major floods occur. It remains a flood by which all others are compared; although, by now, in many places, its record levels have been broken. It also remains a flood that contains many lessons to be learned—if people are willing to listen.

NOTES

Introduction

1. Church, *Flood on White River*.

Chapter 1

2. The Wabash River formed the downstate border between Illinois and Indiana until the flood of June 2008, when the river carved a new channel and created an island of 1,700 acres at the southwestern tip of the state of Indiana. Geographers expect the oxbow of the river's original path to dry up so that these 1,700 acres of Indiana will lie on the other side of the Wabash River. As the journalist noted, "The land's reshaping supplies a lesson in the power of a river to change lives, play havoc with tax and title records, and shake a citizenry's grasp of geography." Jeff Swiatek, "Changing Channels," *Indianapolis Star* (hereafter *IS*), September 11, 2008.
3. Madison, *Indiana Way*, 82–86; Harstad, "Art of Adjustment," 169.
4. Fatout, *Canals*, 76.
5. Harstad, "Art of Adjustment," 169.
6. Madison, *Indiana Way*, 82–86.
7. Lindsey, Crankshaw and Qadir, "Soil Relations," 159.
8. Indiana General Assembly, *Senate Journal* (Indianapolis: J.P. Chapman, 1853), 615.
9. Vileisis, *Unknown Landscape*, 347.
10. Strausberg, "Swamp Lands Act," 191–203.
11. Vileisis, *Unknown Landscape*, 84.

12. Campbell, *Report*, 7, 14–23. My research of the state's landscape and drainage history was made possible by funding from the Environmental Resilience Institute at Indiana University.

13. Whitten, "Address," 19; Indiana Department of Conservation, "Kankakee Basin," 4–5.

14. Ibid., 31–33.

15. Meinig, "The Beholding Eye," 33–47.

16. Dunn, *Greater Indianapolis*, 1:8.

17. Merrill, *Life and Letters*, 13.

18. Dunn, *Greater Indianapolis*, 1:8–14.

19. Hurty, "Indiana's Water Supply," 11.

20. Kershner, "History of Indianapolis," 251–52.

21. Demas McFarland, *Locomotive*, June 13, 1859, quoted in Dunn, *Greater Indianapolis*, 1:10.

22. Dunn, *Greater Indianapolis*, 1:11.

23. Dunn, *Greater Indianapolis*, 1:11–13; Divita, "Workers' Church," 17.

24. Dunn, *Greater Indianapolis*, 1:13.

25. Ibid., 1:13–14.

26. Ibid., 1:14.

27. Ibid.

28. Germano, "White River," 4–5.

29. O'Harrow, "Flood Damage."

30. Jordan, "Concept and Method," 15.

Chapter 2

31. Bybee and Malott, "Flood of 1913," 126–27.

32. Bradsby, *History of Vigo County*, 416–20.

33. Ibid., 433, 454, 459–61.

34. "Relief is Given Indiana Victims of the Tornado," *Indianapolis News* (hereafter *IN*), March 24, 1913; Terre Haute Publishing Company, *Tornado and Flood Disaster*, pages not numbered. A list of the seventeen people who died as a result of the tornado, along with their ages, occupations and addresses, is included in *Terre Haute's Tornado and Flood Disaster*. This list does not include those who died in Terre Haute as a result of the flood, which has been reported as four people.

35. Terre Haute Publishing Company, *Tornado and Flood Disaster*, pages not numbered.

36. As of this writing, the 1913 flood remains the highest crest in Terre Haute's history; although, other floods have come close, most notably the floods of 1958 and 2005. For information about historic and recent crests, see the National Weather Service statistics at www.water.weather.gov.

37. Terre Haute Publishing Company, *Tornado and Flood Disaster*, pages not numbered.

38. Ibid.

39. Bodurtha, *History of Miami County*, 1:157, 1:247–48.

40. Ibid., 1:250, 1:399–401.

41. Ibid., 1:403–4.

42. Marshall, *True Story*, 197.

43. Bodurtha, *History of Miami County*, 1:405–7; Everett, *Tragic Story*, 63–66.

44. Everett, *Tragic Story*, 67–76; Marshall, *True Story*, 198–99; Prochnow, Herbert, Miller and Russell, *Flood and Tornado Calamity*, 173–74; "Elephants Fight Each Other as They Drown," *IN*, March 29, 1913.

45. Bodurtha, ed., *History of Miami County*, 1:405–7; Marshall, *True Story*, 201–3. Reports of the number of people who died in Peru vary greatly—from three in the U.S. Department of Agriculture report, edited by Alfred J. Henry, to eleven in Arthur L. Bodurtha's account (which includes the names and details of how and where they died) and twenty-five in Logan Marshall's book.

46. Grant, "Rivers Meet," 1:379, 1:381; Helm, ed., *History of Allen County*, 90; R.S. Robertson, "Period of Civilization and Law," in *History of Allen County*, edited by T.B. Helm, 44–45.

47. Grant, "Rivers Meet," 1:380; Helm, ed., *History of Allen County*, 56–57; Shoaff, "Floods," 1:415.

48. Shoaff, "Floods," 1:415–17. As of this writing, the 1913 flood remains the highest crest in Fort Wayne's history, although other floods have come close—most notably, the floods of 1982 and 1985. For information about historic and recent crests, see the National Weather Service statistics at www.water.weather.gov.

49. Shoaff, "Floods," 1:416–19; Marshall, *True Story*, 183; Allen County, Indiana Genealogy, "1913 Flood in Fort Wayne, Allen County, Indiana," www.acgsi.org; "Four Orphans Drown When Rescue Boat Turns," *Fort Wayne Gazette* (hereafter *FWG*), March 27, 1913.

50. Shoaff, "Floods," 1:416–19; Marshall, *True Story*, 183; Allen County, Indiana Genealogy, "1913 Flood"; "Safeguarding the Water Supply," *Fort Wayne Sentinel* (hereafter *FWS*), March 26, 1913; "Snow and Ice Add to Terrors of the Floods Which Continue to Increase in Volume; Four Babies Dead," *FWG*, March 27, 1913.

51. R.L. Polk & Company, *Polk's Indianapolis City Directory for 1906* (Southfield, MI: R.L. Polk and Company), 75.

52. Kershner, "History of Indianapolis," 261–62; *Encyclopedia of Indianapolis*, s.v., "Urban Environment," by Philip V. Scarpino.

53. Sackett, "A Sanitary Survey," 112.

54. Tina Jones, Meg Storrow, Paul Diebold and Amy Walker, "Indianapolis Park & Boulevard System," National Register of Historic Places Registration Form, September 18, 2002, Section 8, 4 and 19. Indiana Division of Historic Preservation and Archaeology.

55. Norquest, "Flood," 72.

56. "Part of Meridian Street Bridge is Swept Out," *IN*, March 26, 1913; Marshall, *True Story*, 185–86.

57. Members of the Mary Rigg Senior Citizens Group, "Early West Indianapolis," Special Collections, West Indianapolis Branch, Indianapolis–Marion County Public Library, October 22, 1979, 5.

58. "Belt Railroad Track Reported Washed Out," *IN*, March 26, 1913.

59. Divita, "Workers' Church," 18; "Food Vultures Arouse Markey," *IS*, March 30, 1913.

60. "Reports of Bodies Seen on the Water," *IN*, March 26, 1913.

61. "Two Bridges Are Wrecked; Boulevard is Broken," *IS*, March 26, 1913.

62. "West Washington Bridge Gives Way," *IN*, March 26, 1913.

63. Prochnow, Herbert, Miller and Russell, *Flood and Tornado Calamity*, 171–72; "Known West Side Dead," *IN*, March 27, 1913; "Men Thought Drowned Are Discovered Safe," *IN*, March 28, 1913; "Boy Is Killed by Live Wire in Flood District," *IN*, March 29, 1913; "Local Flood Victims," *IN*, March 31, 1913.

64. B.F. Bowen and Company Inc., *History of Lawrence and Monroe Counties*, 25–28, 67–75, 176, 193, 206–7, 210–12. The site where the town of Palestine once stood was abandoned, and at the time of Bowen's publication in 1914, the former site was a meadow with a grove of trees standing on the hill. All traces of the former town and its inhabitants have been erased, unless one digs below the soil to find remaining relics, including bricks from the courthouse. The explanation for malaria outbreaks were blamed on "miasma," but opinions varied as to whether the miasma originated from the river, the tan yard behind the town, the frequent dense fogs, the Native American burial ground on which the town sat or the town water supply, which came from a spring below the burial ground.

65. B.F. Bowen and Company Inc., *History of Lawrence and Monroe Counties*, 150–53, 193–204.

66. Ibid., 180–92.

67. B.F. Bowen and Company Inc., *History of Lawrence and Monroe Counties*, 25–27; "Deluge of Rain Monday Night Swells Streams to Flood Stage," *BDM*, March 25, 1913; Silver Jackets, "Great Flood."

68. "Greatest Flood Known in History of Ohio Valley: All High Water Marks are Being Smashed," *BDM*, March 26, 1913; "Strenuous Efforts Being Made to Save Oldest Bridge," *BDM*, March 26, 1913; B.F. Bowen and Company Inc., *History of Lawrence and Monroe Counties*, 57–58.

69. "Rawlins Bridge Settled Back One Inch Out of Line," *BDM*, March 31, 1913; National Weather Service, "East Fork White River at Bedford Boat Club," www. water.weather.gov. The 1913 crest of 47.5 feet was the highest historic crest; the second highest historic crest occurred on January 24, 1937, at 37.20 feet.

70. Shaw, ed., *History of Dearborn County*, 1:230–38; Shaw, ed., *History of Dearborn County*, 2:1062.

71. Shaw, *History of Dearborn County*, 1:243–49, 1:488.

72. Ibid., 1:491–98.

73. Ibid., 1:498–504.

74. Shaw, *History of Dearborn County*, 1:498–504; Marshall, *True Story*, 265.

75. Marshall, *True Story*, 191–95; "Leland P. Woolery Drowned at Lafayette," *MRT,* March 27, 1913.

76. "Two Men Floated Out on Crossties," *BDM*, March 31, 1913.

77. "Tornado and Flood Cause Big Damage," *Richmond Palladium* (hereafter *RP*), March 24, 1913; "Region of Happy Hollow Now Most Desolated Part of City— People Homeless," *RP,* March 25, 1913; "Summary of Damage Flood Did in County," *RP,* March 25, 1913; "Piano Company's Factory Flooded," *RP,* March 25, 1913; "North End Shows Effects of Flood in Broken Bridges," *Richmond Evening Item*, March 26, 1913.

78. "Lowlands of County Are Underwater," "Mississinewa Leaves Banks Near Marion" and "Union City Is Marooned," *Muncie Evening Press* (hereafter *MEP*), March 24, 1913; "Angry River Claims One Victim; Watchman on Bridge Drowned," *MEP,* March 25, 1913; "Floods Begin to Recede on Tuesday Night," *MEP*, March 26, 1913.

79. "Estimate Loss in City $250,000," "Rushville Cut Off from World," "Damage Seen from Tower," "James Hubbard Drowned Today" and "Loss Cannot Be Estimated Now," *Jacksonian-Republican* (hereafter *JR*), March 25, 1913; "All Past Records are Shattered" and "City Loss Heavy from the Water," *JR*, March 26, 1913.

80. "Twelve Lives Lost; Immense Loss of Property," *Brookville Democrat* (hereafter *BD*), March 28, 1913; "Flood's Death Toll Is Fifteen," *BD*, April 3, 1913; "Four Caskets," *BD*, April 3, 1913; "Two More Bodies Found," *BD*, April 9, 1913.

81. "Hard Rains Turned Streets into Rivers," *Martinsville Reporter-Times* (hereafter *MRT*), March 24, 1913; "White River on a Rampage" and "Special Meeting of City Council," *MRT*, March 25, 1913; "Immense Damage from Great Flood," *MRT*, March 26, 1913; "Flood Conditions Are Improving," *MRT*, March 28, 1913.

82. "Columbus Isolated by Worst Flood Reported Since Freshet of 1898," *Columbus Republican* (hereafter *CR*), March 27, 1913; "Fifty Thousand Is About Sum Required" and "Indianapolis Sends Mayor Offer of Aid," *CR*, April 3, 1913.

83. "Greatest Flood," *BDM*; "Vincennes Damaged $500,000," *BDM*, March 29, 1913; "Vincennes Suffers," *FWS*, March 29, 1913; "Tents Were Sent by State to Shoals and Vincennes to Shelter Refugees," *BDM*, April 1, 1913.

84. "Indiana Flood: Wabash and White Rivers Are Doing Much Damage Near Their Mouths," *BDM*, April 1, 1913.

85. "Indiana Flood," *BDM*; "High Waves Splash Against Buildings on Water Street," *Evansville Press* (hereafter *EP*), April 2, 1913; "Evansville Flood Told in a Nutshell" and "Firing of Shots Gives Warning of Cutting of Levee," *EP*, April 4, 1913; "Ohio River on Stand; Further Danger Is Over," *EP*, April 5, 1913; "River Falls Slowly on the Local Gauge [*sic*]," *EP*, April 8, 1913; National Weather Service, "Ohio River at Evansville," www.water.weather.gov.

86. "Flood Conditions," *MRT*; "Hundreds Will Return as Paupers to Farms," *EP*, April 4, 1913; "Must Have Big Loan to Assist Many Farmers," *EP*, April 8, 1913; "Will Ask for $200,000 to Reimburse Flood Sufferers," *EP*, April 14, 1913; "$63,000 Will Be Spent Nearby for Flood Sufferers," *EP*, April 24, 1913.

87. "Salt Creek Drowned Families in Brown County," *BDM*, March 28, 1913.

88. "Seventeen Houses in Shoals Have Been Washed Away" and "Sixteen Deaths at Evansville," *BDM*, March 29, 1913.

89. "General Story of the Great Wilson Flood," *BDM*, March 29, 1913.

90. See, for example, "Most Disastrous Flood in Years Paralyzes People Throughout Ohio and Hoosier State," *SBT*, March 25, 1913; "8,000 People in Dayton Are Victims of a Catastrophe; News Is Difficult to Secure," *RP*, March 25, 1913; "5,000 Dead in Dayton, Late Toll," *IS*, March 26, 1913.

91. "Aged Couple Were Unharmed," *Jacksonian-Republican*, March 26, 1913.

92. "Lives Lost," *BD*; "Bodies Found," *BD*.

93. "Marooned Train Crew Reached This City Today from Oolitic," *BDM*, March 28, 1913.

94. "Stork Makes Visit as Family Leave Home in Boat," *BDM*, March 31, 1913.

95. "Man With Nude Body Spent Night in Tree," *CR*, April 3, 1913.

96. "Six Babies Born to Peru Flood Refugees," *IN*, March 27, 1913.

97. "Incidents of the Flood," *IN*, March 28, 1913.

98. "White River," *MRT*.

99. "Caught in Swirling Mass of the Flood," *IN*, March 27, 1913.

100. "Waters of Indiana Floods Receding," *IN*, March 26, 1913.

101. "Edward N. Giblett Assists in Rescue," *SBT*, March 28, 1913.

102. See, for example, United Press, "500 May Be Drowned at Peru, Says Fleming," "Corpses Float Down the Streets of Peru" and "Death List at Peru May Amount to 150," *EP*, March 28, 1913; Associated Press, "Day Breaks Over Desolation: Slight Hope Retained That the First Estimates of Loss of Life May Have Been Exaggerated," *Richmond Evening Item*, March 26, 1913; "Many Wild Stories," *BDM*, March 28, 1913.

103. "West Side Dead," *IN*; "Drowning of William Geyer" and "Drastic Steps Taken to Prevent Looting," *IN*, March 27, 1913; "Men Thought Drowned Are Discovered Safe" and "Much Distress Over Many Missing People," *IN*, March 28, 1913.

104. Norquest, "Flood," 71–72, 74. The U.S. Inflation Calculator indicates that $20 million in 1913 would have been equal to $518 million in 2020.

Chapter 3

105. W.M. Herschell, "Raging Waters Disprove Old Theories of Man's Inhumanity to Man, Citizens of High and Low Degree Joining Hands to Aid the Homeless," *IN*, March 29, 1913.

106. Mount Vernon, Indiana, Relief Association, Relief in Mount Vernon 1913, publisher not specified, 1913, no page numbers.

107. Marshall, *True Story*, 187–88.

108. General Relief Committee, *Report*, 12–13.

109. Reverend Weber quoted in Divita, "Workers' Church," 23; Divita, "Workers' Church," 17–20; Wolfer, "Social History," 3.

110. Haine, interview, 13–14.

111. "Masons Load a Car with Supplies for the Needy," *IN*, March 28, 1913.

112. "Offer of Aid," *CR*.

113. "Rome City News," *FWG*, March 27, 1913; "South Bend Meat" and "Pathetic Stories," *FWS*, March 28, 1913; "Mishawaka Sends Aid," *SBT*, March 27, 1913.

114. General Relief Committee, *Report*, 12–13, 31–33, 40; "Rush of Money to News Flood Fund," *IN*, March 27, 1913; Habbe, "Indianapolis Flood of 1913."

115. "Governor Ralston Reviews Indiana Flood Relief," *BDM*, April 17, 1913.

116. "General Story," *BDM*.

117. "Wilson Sends a Message to Ralston," *IN*, March 26, 1913.

118. See, for example, "U.S. Holds Troops Ready; Starts Food and Tents to Flood Victims," *MRT*, March 26, 1913.

119. President Woodrow Wilson, quoted in "Wilson Issues an Appeal for Aid," *FWG*, March 27, 1913.

120. "Asks Government to Send Medical Expert," *IN*, March 27, 1913; "Red Cross Official Here" and "Ambulance Company Is Ordered to Peru's Aid," *IN*, April 3, 1913.

121. "Medical Expert," *IN*.

122. "Supt. Hyland Placed in Active Command," *IN*, March 29, 1913.

123. "Ambulance Company," *IN*.

124. "Would Wipe Town of Taylorsville [*sic*] Off Map," *IN*, April 4, 1913. Note that the town referred to in Vigo County is Taylorville. The town of Taylorsville is located in Bartholomew County.

125. "Vaccine or Starve, Order," *CR*, April 10, 1913.

126. "Flood Prevention Worrying Wilson," *CR*, April 10, 1913.

127. "Barn in Public Highway" and "New White House Has Lodged in Tree South Sparksville," *BDM*, April 1, 1913; "Finds Dynamite in House," *Scott County Journal*, April 9, 1913.

128. General Relief Committee, *Report*, 12–13.

129. "Notes of the Flood" and "Said He Had Counted At Least Fifty Bodies," *IN*, March 28, 1913.

130. Marshall, *True Story*, 189; "Vaccination Free" and "Statement Is Given Out by Dr. T.V. Keene," *IN*, March 28, 1913; A.W. Brayton, "Typhoid Vaccination," *IN*, March 31, 1913.

131. Hoy, *Chasing Dirt*, 65, 86.

132. "A Reason Sanitary Measures Are Necessary," *IN*, March 29, 1913.

133. Common Council of the City of Indianapolis, Indiana, *Journals of the Common Council of the City of Indianapolis, Indiana, from January 1, 1913, to January 5, 1914* (Indianapolis: Sentinel Printing Company, 1914), 216–17. The mayor of Indianapolis approved General Ordinance No. 34 on August 21, 1913, after the ordinance was amended to restrict each patrolman's inspection and reporting responsibilities to his own district. By the time of approval, the language regarding the existence of an emergency was struck.

134. "Governor Hears About Pesthole," *IN*, April 5, 1913; "Hurty Gives Orders About Taylorville" and "May Take Command of Taylorville Situation," *IN*, April 11, 1913; W.M. Herschell, "Taylorville, On the Wabash, Unworthy of a Place on the Map, Turns from Flood to Engage in Battle with the Sanitarians," *IN*, April 12, 1913. Taylorville remains an unincorporated area that also goes by the name of Dresser.

135. "Men Repair Their Homes," *IN*, March 28, 1913.

136. "West Indianapolis Brighter and in Better Condition Than Ever Before Despite Its Privations; On the First Anniversary of Its Great Flood," *IN*, March 21, 1914; Wolfer, quoting a local resident in "Social History," 3.

137. Marshall, *True Story*, 188; "Proclamation of Martial Law Ready," *IN*, March 27, 1913.

138. "Proclamation," *IN*.

139. "Destruction Left in Wake of Flood," *MEP*, March 26, 1913; "Indiana Flood," *BDM*.

140. "Fighting Loan Shark Evil," *MRT*, April 3, 1913.

141. Marshall, *True Story*, 188–89; "Proclamation," *IN*; "Police to Keep Eye on the Food Prices," *IN*, March 28, 1913; "Food Vultures," *IS*.

142. See, for example, "Women in Charge of Relief Work Are Proving to Be Real Heroines," *FWG*, March 29, 1913.

143. "Wrecked; Broken," *IS*, March 26, 1913.

144. "Hundreds Visited Waverly Sunday," *MRT*, March 31, 1913.

145. "Sees Crisis Upon State," *FWS*, March 27, 1913; "Floods Delay Paychecks," *IN*, March 31, 1913; "Teachers Examination Saturday," *BDM*, April 3, 1913.

146. "Escaped Waters for One Season," *FWS*, March 28, 1913.

147. "Newlyweds Are Carried Through Flooded Streets," *EP*, April 3, 1913.

148. See, for example, "Flood Photos," *BD*, April 3, 1913; "Flood Pictures" and "The Flood," *BD*, April 30, 1913; "A Great Flood of Business," *FWG*, March 27, 1913; "The Boston Store: To Flood Victims," *FWS*, March 31, 1913.

149. "Vote 'Dry' at Delphi," *IN*, March 28, 1913; "Voters 'Dry' in Spite of Floods," *FWG*, March 27, 1913; "Princeton 'Dry' Despite Flood," *EP*, April 3, 1913; "'Wet' Majority in Goshen Is Reduced," *CR*, April 10, 1913; "Laurel Goes 'Wet,'" *BD*, April 30, 1913.

150. State Board of Tax Commissioners, "Notice," *BD*, April 23, 1913.

151. "Flood Uncovers an Old Burying Ground," *CR*, April 3, 1913.

152. "Floatsam and Jetsam," *MEP*, March 26, 1913.

Chapter 4

153. Chris Robbins, "A Brief History of Weather Forecasting," iWeatherNet.com, January 17, 2015, www.iweathernet.com.

154. Shoaff, "Floods," 1:416, referring to reports in the *FWG* and *Fort Wayne Weekly Sentinel*, respectively, following these events.

155. "The Flood and Its Lessons," *FWS*, March 31, 1913.

156. Germano, "'Dangerous Friends,'" 89–90. Major floods in 1915 and 1916 prompted the passage of the first federal Flood Control Act of 1917, which President Wilson signed to appropriate $45 million for U.S. Army Corps of Engineer projects on the Mississippi and Sacramento Rivers.

157. Everett, *Tragic Story*, 228; "Do You Know This Year's Flood Loss Would Pay for Flood Control?" *EP*, April 5, 1913.

158. "Board Decides to Improve the River," *IN*, April 4, 1913; Germano, "View of the Valley," 42–44. At the time of statehood and by early–nineteenth century standards, using canoes and flatboats, the Wabash River and many of its tributaries were navigable. In *Ross, et al. v. Faust, et al.*, 54 Ind. 471 (1876), a case involving two riparian property owners arguing over the right to take gravel from the bed of White River in front of Ross's property, the Indiana Supreme Court proclaimed the White River a non-navigable river. It was not until 1950 that the Indiana Supreme Court questioned the 1876 ruling and reinstated White River to its legally recognized navigable status. See *State ex rel. Indiana Department of Conservation v. Kivett*, 95 N.E.2d 145 (Ind. Supreme Court 1950).

159. "Brighter and in Better Condition," *IN*.

160. "Board Decides," *IN*.

161. Shoaff, "Floods," 1:417. See another article in the series—for example, Frank B. Taylor, "Frank B. Taylor Reviews Causes of the Flood and Possible Measures Against Its Recurrence," *FWS*, April 12, 1913.

162. O.N. Guldlin, "The Lessons of the Flood," *FWS*, March 31, 1913.

163. "New River Channel Would Lessen Floods," *MEP*, March 29, 1913; Helm, "Center Township" and "Munseytown—The Seat of Justice," in *History of Delaware County*.

164. "Flood Gates and Pumps Are to Be Installed," *EP*, April 2, 1913.

165. "Relief Fund," "Commercial Club" and "Vice President," *BD*, April 16, 1913.

166. "County Ought to Purchase Motor Boats," *MEP*, March 26, 1913; "Angry River," *MEP*.

167. Everett, *Tragic Story*, 77–97.

168. Shoaff, "Floods," 1:417–19.

169. National Weather Service, "Evansville"; Welky, *Thousand-Year Flood*, 229.

170. Galloway, "Corps of Engineers Responses," 6; Holmes, Koenig and Karstensen, "Flooding in the United States," 1–3; Morlock, Menke, Arvin and Kim, "Flood of June 7–9, 2008."

BIBLIOGRAPHY

Batic, Eloise, and Angela Giacomelli. "Wulf's Hall: Great Hope in the Midst of the Great Flood." *Traces of Indiana and Midwestern History* 25, no. 2 (Spring 2013): 4–11.

Beatty, John D., ed. *History of Fort Wayne & Allen County, Indiana.* Vol. 1. Evansville, IN: M.T. Publishing Company Inc., 2006.

Bell, Trudy E. "Indiana's Great Easter Flood of 1913: Forgotten Waters." *Traces of Indiana and Midwestern History* 18, no. 2 (Spring 2006): 4–15.

B.F. Bowen and Company Inc. *History of Lawrence and Monroe Counties, Indiana: Their People, Industries, and Institutions.* Indianapolis: B.F. Bowen and Company Inc., 1914. www.archive.org.

Bodurtha, Arthur L., ed. *History of Miami County, Indiana: A Narrative Account of Its Historical Progress and Its Principal Interests.* Vol. 1. Chicago: Lewis Publishing Company, 1914. www.archive.org.

Bradsby, H.C. *History of Vigo County, Indiana, with Biographical Selections.* 1891. Reprint, Evansville, IN: Unigraphic, Inc., 1969. www.archive.org.

Bybee, Hal P., and Clyde A. Malott. "The Flood of 1913 in the Lower White River Region of Indiana." *Indiana University Studies: Contribution to Knowledge Made by Instructors and Advanced Students of the University* 2, no. 22 (October 1914): 105–223. www.babel.hathitrust.org.

Campbell, John L. *Report Upon the Improvement of the Kankakee River and the Drainage of the Marshlands in Indiana to the Governor.* Indianapolis: William B. Burford, State Printer, 1883. www.babel.hathitrust.org.

Church, Verne H., section director. Department of Agriculture, Weather Bureau. *The Flood on White River in March 1913.* Indianapolis, April 8, 1913.

Divita, James J. "Workers' Church: Centennial History of the Catholic Parish of the Assumption of the Blessed Virgin Mary in West Indianapolis." Indianapolis: Centennial Committee, Church of the Assumption, 1994.

BIBLIOGRAPHY

Dunn, Jacob Piatt. *Greater Indianapolis: The History, the Industries, the Institutions, and the People of a City of Homes*. Chicago: Lewis Publishing Company, 1910.

Esarey, Logan. *A History of Indiana: From Its Exploration to 1850*. Indianapolis: Hoosier Heritage Press Inc., 1970.

Everett, Marshall. *Tragic Story of America's Greatest Disaster: Tornado, Flood and Fire in Ohio, Indiana, Nebraska and Mississippi Valley*. Chicago: J.S. Ziegler Company, 1913. www.books.google.com.

Fatout, Paul. *Indiana Canals*. West Lafayette, IN: Purdue University Studies, 1972.

Galloway, Gerald E., Jr. "Corps of Engineers Responses to the Changing National Approach to Floodplain Management Since the 1993 Midwest Flood." *Journal of Contemporary Water Research & Education* 130 (March 2005): 5–12. www.opensiuc.lib.siu.edu.

General Relief Committee. *The Report of the Indianapolis General Relief Committee for Flood Sufferers, Appointed by Mayor Samuel Lewis Shank, March 26, 1913*. Indianapolis: Cornelius Printing Company, 1913.

Germano, Nancy M. "The Urban Midwest's 'Dangerous Friends': At the Confluence of Flooding Rivers, An Environmental Movement, And a National Insurance Program." PhD diss., Indiana University, 2017.

———. "A View of the Valley: The 1913 Flood in West Indianapolis." Master's thesis, Indiana University, 2009.

———. "White River and the 'Great Flood' of 1913: An Environmental History of Indianapolis." *Circular* (Winter 2008): 1–7.

Grant, Jane A. "Where the Rivers Meet: An Ecological History of Fort Wayne & Allen County." In *History of Fort Wayne & Allen County, Indiana*. Edited by John D. Beatty. Vol. 1. Evansville, IN: M.T. Publishing Company Inc., 2006, 378–87.

Habbe, Edith. "The Indianapolis Flood of 1913: A Study of Disaster and Permanent Dependency Based on 2,332 Families Receiving Rehabilitation Aid After the 1913 Flood." Master's thesis, Indiana University, 1920.

Haine, Adeline Claghorn. "1913 Flood (West Indianapolis, Indiana) 523 Coffey Street, As Remembered by Adeline Claghorn Haine in 1979." Interviewed by Vicki Haine Hatfield. Adeline Claghorn Haine, 2000.

Harstad, Peter T. "Indiana and the Art of Adjustment." In *Heartland: Comparative Histories of the Midwestern States*. Edited by James H. Madison. Bloomington: Indiana University Press, 1988, 158–85.

Helm, T.B., ed. *History of Allen County, Indiana, with Illustrations and Biographical Sketches of Some of Its Prominent Men and Pioneers*. Chicago: Kingman Brothers, 1880. www.archive.org.

———. *History of Delaware County, Indiana*. 1881. Reprint, Evansville, IN: Unigraphic Inc., 1976. www.freepages.rootsweb.com.

Henry, Alfred J., U.S. Department of Agriculture, Weather Bureau. *The Floods of 1913 in the Rivers of the Ohio and Lower Mississippi Valleys*. Washington, D.C.: Government Printing Office, 1913. www.archive.org.

Holmes, Robert L., Jr., Todd A. Koenig and Krista A. Karstensen. "Flooding in the United States Midwest, 2008." U.S. Department of the Interior, U.S. Geological Survey, professional paper, 1775. Reston, VA: U.S. Geological Survey, 2010. www.pubs.usgs.gov.

Howard, Timothy Edward. *A History of St. Joseph County, Indiana*. Vol. 1. Chicago: Lewis Publishing Company, 1907. www.archive.org.

Hoy, Suellen. *Chasing Dirt: The American Pursuit of Cleanliness*. New York: Oxford University Press, 1995.

Hurty, John N. "History of Indiana's Water Supply." In *Conference of Municipal and Private Owned Water Plants of Indiana with the State Board of Health at Indianapolis, July 8 and 9, 1908*. Indianapolis: William B. Burford, 1908, 7–17. www.archive.org.

Indiana Department of Conservation. "The Kankakee Basin Plan." Isaak Walton League of America, 1942.

Indianapolis General Relief Committee for Flood Sufferers, March 26, 1913, to December 29, 1913, appointed by Mayor Samuel Lewis Shank March 26, 1913, and disbanded upon the completion of its duties December 29, 1913. *The Indianapolis Flood of March 1913, And Measures for Relief of Flood Victims*. Indianapolis: Cornelius Printing Company, n.d.

Jordan, Terry G. "The Concept and Method." In *Regional Studies: The Interplay of Land and People*. Edited by Glen E. Lich. College Station: Texas A&M University Press, 1992, 8–24.

Kemper, J.P. *Rebellious River: Use and Abuse of America's Natural Resources*. 1949. Reprint, New York: Arno Press, 1972.

Kershner, Frederick Doyle, Jr. "A Social and Cultural History of Indianapolis, 1860–1914." PhD diss., University of Wisconsin, 1950.

Lindsey, Alton A., William B. Crankshaw and Syed A. Qadir. "Soil Relations and Distribution Map of the Vegetation of Presettlement Indiana." *Botanical Gazette* 126, no. 3 (September 1965): 155–63.

Madison, James H., ed. *Heartland: Comparative Histories of the Midwestern States*. Bloomington: Indiana University Press, 1988.

———. *The Indiana Way: A State History*. First Midland Book Edition. Bloomington: Indiana University Press, 1990.

Marsh, George P. *The Earth as Modified by Human Action*. New York: Scribner, Armstrong & Co., 1864.

Marshall, Logan. *The True Story of Our National Calamity of Flood, Fire and Tornado: The Appalling Loss of Life, the Terrible Suffering of the Homeless, the Struggles for Safety*. N.p.: L.T. Myers, 1913. www.books.google.com.

Meinig, D.W., ed. "The Beholding Eye: Ten Versions of the Same Scene." In *The Interpretation of Ordinary Landscapes: Geographical Essays*. New York: Oxford University Press, 1979, 33–47.

Members of the Mary Rigg Senior Citizens Group: Malcolm Biggs, Esther Cauble, George James, Marcella James, Ernest Leawellen, Genevieve Repass, William

Reuter, Lorena Totton and Leland Winsted. "Early West Indianapolis." Special Collections, West Indianapolis Branch, Indianapolis–Marion County Public Library, October 22, 1979.

Merrill, Catharine. *Catharine Merrill: Life and Letters.* Collected and arranged by Katharine Merrill Graydon. Greenfield, IN: The Mitchell Company, 1934.

Morlock, Scott E., Chad D. Menke, Donald V. Arvin and Moon H. Kim. U.S. Geological Survey, Open-File Report 2008-1322, "Flood of June 7–9, 2008, in Central and Southern Indiana." www.pubs.usgs.gov.

Mount Vernon, Indiana, Charity Association. *Relief in Mt. Vernon 1913.* N.p., 1913.

Newspapers. www.newspapers.com.

Norquest, C.E. "Flood in the White River of Indiana, March 1913." In *The Floods of 1913 in the Rivers of the Ohio and Lower Mississippi Valleys.* Washington, D.C.: Government Printing Office, 1913, 71–4. www.archive.org.

O'Harrow, Dennis. State Planning Board of Indiana. "Indiana Flood Damage." February 1937.

Prochnow, Herbert Victor, Thomas Herbert, J. Martin Miller and Thomas Herbert Russell. *America's Greatest Flood and Tornado Calamity, Authentic Stories of These Appalling Disasters.* Ann Arbor: University of Michigan, 1913. www.books.google.com.

R.L. Polk & Company. *Polk's City Directory of Indianapolis.* Microfilm Collection. Indiana State Library.

Sackett, R.L. "A Sanitary Survey of White River from Winchester to Martinsville, Indiana." In *Proceedings of the Twenty-Seventh Annual Meeting of the Indiana Engineering Society held at Indianapolis, January 17, 18, 19, 1907.* Indianapolis: Indiana Engineering Society, 1907, 100–13. www.babel.hathitrust.org.

Shaw, Archibald, ed. *History of Dearborn County, Indiana: Her People, Industries, and Institutions, with Bibliographical Sketches of Representative Citizens and Genealogical Records of Old Families.* Vol. 1. 1915. Reprint, Evansville, IN: Unigraphic Inc., 1980. www.archive.org.

———. *History of Dearborn County, Indiana: Her People, Industries, and Institutions, With Bibliographical Sketches of Representative Citizens and Genealogical Records of Old Families.* Vol. 2. 1915. Indianapolis: B.F. Bowen and Company Inc., 1915. www.archive.org.

Shoaff, John H. "Fort Wayne's Floods." In *History of Fort Wayne & Allen County, Indiana.* Vol. 1. Edited by John D. Beatty. Evansville, IN: M.T. Publishing Company Inc., 2006, 415–19.

Silver Jackets. "The Great Flood of 1913, 100 Years Later: Community Profiles." www.mrcc.illinois.edu.

Strausberg, Stephen F. "Indiana and the Swamp Lands Act: A Study in State Administration." *Indiana Magazine of History* 73, no. 3 (September 1977): 191–203.

Terre Haute Publishing Company. *Terre Haute's Tornado and Flood Disaster, March Twenty-Third to March Thirtieth, Nineteen Hundred and Thirteen, Containing a Graphic Description of the Appalling Events as They Transpired and Showing Views of the Destruction Wrought by the Terrible Catastrophe.* Terre Haute, IN: Viquesney Company, n.d.

BIBLIOGRAPHY

U.S. Congress. *Abstract of the Returns of the Fifth Census, Showing the Number of Free People, the Number of Slaves, the Federal or Representative Number, and the Aggregate of Each County of Each State of the United States.* Twenty-Second Congress, first session, 1831–1833. H. Doc. 269. www2.census.gov.

Vileisis, Ann. *Discovering the Unknown Landscape: A History of America's Wetlands.* Washington, D.C.: Island Press, 1999.

Welky, David. *The Thousand-Year Flood: The Ohio-Mississippi Disaster of 1937.* Chicago: University of Chicago Press, 2011.

Whitten, William M. "Address by President Whitten." In *Proceedings of the Fourteenth Annual Meeting of the Indiana Engineering Society held at Indianapolis, Indiana, January 2, 3 and 4, 1894.* South Bend, IN: Tribune Printing Company, 1895, 14–26. www. babel.hathitrust.org.

Wolfer, Margaret. "Social History of the 'West Indianapolis' Section of Indianapolis, Indiana." Special Collections, West Indianapolis Branch, Indianapolis–Marion County Public Library, 1970s.

INDEX

INDEX

T

U

V

W

ABOUT THE AUTHOR

Nancy M. Germano is an instructor of history at Butler University. She earned her doctorate in history, with a research focus on flooding and environmental history in the Midwest, from Indiana University.

www.ingramcontent.com/pod-product-compliance
Lightning Source LLC
Chambersburg PA
CBHW070335100426
42812CB00005B/1336